EDIT YOURSELF

Also by Bruce Ross-Larson

In Hardcover

Effective Writing: Stunning Sentences,
Powerful Paragraphs, and Riveting Reports

Writing for the Information Age:
Elements of Style for the Twenty-First Century

In Paperback

Powerful Paragraphs

Riveting Reports

Stunning Sentences

Edit Yourself

A Manual for Everyone
Who Works with Words

by BRUCE ROSS-LARSON

W. W. Norton & Company
New York - London

© 1996, 1982, by Bruce Ross-Larson

Printed in the United States of America.

First published as a Norton paperback 1985;
reissued with new material 1996

Library of Congress Cataloging-in-Publication Data

Ross-Larson, Bruce Clifford, 1942–
    Edit yourself.
    1. English language—Rhetoric.   2. English
language—Grammar—1950   3. Authorship—
Handbooks, manuals, etc.   4. Editing.   I. Title.
PE1408.R725   1982   808'.042   82-6432
                                AACR2

ISBN 0-393-31326-3

W. W. Norton & Company, Inc.
500 Fifth Avenue, New York, N.Y. 10110
W. W. Norton & Company Ltd.
10 Coptic Street, London WC1A 1PU

    7 8 9 0

TO GODDARD WINTERBOTTOM
for showing the way

Contents

Author's Note

In the first part of this book I have drawn together solutions to the more common problems of everyday writing, such problems as fat, inconsistency, and the failure to use parallel grammatical constructions. In the second part I have arranged, in alphabetical order, more than 1,500 common cuts, changes, and comparisons that editors make to produce clear, concise writing. The recommendations in that part enlarge on the solutions proposed in the first two chapters of part I: "Fat" and "The Better Word." Those recommendations would, I admit, reduce great prose to the ordinary. But if followed, they can lift ordinary writing to a plane of greater clarity and distinction.

Bruce Ross-Larson

Acknowledgments

For suggestions about the shape and content of this book and for guidance on many problems of editing, I owe much to Harriet Baldwin, Jane Carroll, Carl Dahlman, George Dorsey, David Driscoll, Richard Herbert, Virginia Hitchcock, Andrea Hodson, David Howell Jones, Starling Lawrence, James McEuen, Ricardo Moran, Marilyn Silverman, Brian Svikhart, Kim Tran, Larry Westphal, Goddard Winterbottom, and especially Edward Hodnett. I also owe much to the books I frequently pull from my shelf: *Merriam-Webster's Collegiate Dictionary*, Strunk and White's *Elements of Style*, Fowler's *Modern English Usage*, Follett's *Modern American Usage*, Gowers's *Complete Plain Words*, Flesch's *ABC of Style*, *The Chicago Manual of Style*, and Prentice-Hall's *Handbook for Writers* and *Words into Type*.

For this second edition I thank my colleagues at Communications Development—Meta de Coquereaumont and Alison Strong for their editorial eyes, and Amy Cracknell and Julie Harris for composing the book and managing the new material.

Part I **WHAT EDITORS
LOOK FOR**

Chapter 1 **Fat**

Just as your speech is filled with many words that add nothing to what you say, your writing is often larded with words that obscure your meaning rather than clarify it. Trim this fat to direct your reader's attention to important words and ideas.

SUPERFLUOUS NOUNS

Superfluous nouns fatten many sentences and distract attention from a stronger noun by relegating it to a prepositional phrase.

the field of economics	CHANGE TO	economics
the level of wages rose	CHANGE TO	wages rose
the process of industrial- ization	CHANGE TO	industrialization
the volume of demand fell	CHANGE TO	demand fell

Such trimming does not always work, but it does work often. Here is a list of nouns that, interposed between *the* and *of,* can often be done away with.

the amount of	CUT
the area of	CUT
the case of	CUT
the character of	CUT

the concept of	CUT
the degree of	CUT
the existence of	CUT
the extent of	CUT
the field of	CUT
the form of	CUT
the idea of	CUT
the level of	CUT
the magnitude of	CUT
the nature of	CUT
the number of	CUT
the presence of	CUT
the process of	CUT
the purpose of	CUT
the sum of	CUT
the volume of	CUT
the way of	CUT

SUPERFLUOUS VERBS

There are two classes of superfluous verb. One is an array of pretenders—idle, common verbs that supplant a working verb, which becomes a noun: such verbs as *do, have, is, make, provide,* and *serve.*

do a study of the effects	CHANGE TO	study the effects
have a tendency to	CHANGE TO	tend to
is indicative of	CHANGE TO	indicates
make changes in	CHANGE TO	change
make decisions about	CHANGE TO	decide on
make progress toward	CHANGE TO	progress toward
provide a summary of	CHANGE TO	summarize
serve to make reductions	CHANGE TO	reduce

This formula changes the objective noun to a verb and displaces the pretender. Take care, however, not to be too zealous in applying this formula, or you will end up with such artificial verbs as *prioritize, concretize,* or *incentivize.*

The second class of superfluous verb is found in clauses that modify nouns. Such verbs, along with the pronouns and helping verbs that precede them, can often be deleted.

the ice that is contained in	CHANGE TO	the ice in
the people who are concerned are	CHANGE TO	the people are
the argument that is included in	CHANGE TO	the argument in
the tasks that are involved in	CHANGE TO	the tasks in
the people who are located in	CHANGE TO	the people in
the numbers shown in	CHANGE TO	the numbers in
the estimates presented in	CHANGE TO	the estimates in
the facts given in	CHANGE TO	the facts in

SUPERFLUOUS ARTICLES AND PREPOSITIONS

the making of cloth	CHANGE TO	making cloth
the manufacture of steel	CHANGE TO	manufacturing steel
many of the countries	CHANGE TO	many countries
several of the countries	CHANGE TO	several countries
some of the countries	CHANGE TO	some countries
fill up the tank	CHANGE TO	fill the tank
lay out the pipes	CHANGE TO	lay the pipes

Note that these recommendations can sometimes change the meaning. If they do, let the original construction stand.

THE OPENING "IT"

Two classes of the opening *It* indicate fat. The first is *It is...*, *It was...*, or *It will be...*, followed by the subject, followed by *who, that,* or *which.* The construction sometimes is justifiable for emphasis, but it generally is unacceptable because it gives the prominent lead position in the sentence to a pronoun not yet defined, a position that the subject deserves. And it takes three additional words.

It is Richard who damaged...	CHANGE TO	Richard damaged...
It was Wang Laboratories that engineered...	CHANGE TO	Wang Laboratories engineered...

The second class is a series of circumlocutions—of uses of many words where fewer will do—that begin with the indefinite pronoun *It*.

It appears that Cuba will...	CHANGE TO	Cuba will...
It goes without saying that I...	CHANGE TO	I...
It should be noted that I...	CHANGE TO	I...

Almost any sentence will be improved by trimming such fatty constructions.

THE OPENING "THERE"

Two classes of the opening *There* should be avoided. The first is the same as the first class of the opening *It*.

There are some buildings that will...	CHANGE TO	Some buildings will...
There are some people who are...	CHANGE TO	Some people are...

The second class relegates what might precede the verb to less prominence after the verb.

There is nothing wrong with the opening *there*, unless there are too many *there*'s in evidence.	CHANGE TO	Nothing is wrong with the opening *there*, unless too many *there*'s are evident.

Note that such rescues are not always felicitous: *There are two reasons* should not be changed to *Reasons are two* or to *Two reasons exist.*

OVERWEIGHT PREPOSITIONS

Many overweight phrases needlessly detract from the object they introduce by fattening a sentence. Here are some samples of phrases that should usually be replaced by shorter prepositions.

as regards	CHANGE TO	on, for, about
as to	CUT OR CHANGE TO	in, of, on, for, about
concerning	CHANGE TO	at, of, on, for, about
in regards to	CHANGE TO	on, about

in relation to	CHANGE TO	on, about
in respect to	CHANGE TO	on, about
in terms of	TRY	as, at, by, in, of, for, with, under, through
regarding	TRY	on, for, about
related to	TRY	of, on, about
relating to	TRY	on, for, about
with reference to	CHANGE TO	of, on, for, about
with respect to	CHANGE TO	on, for, about

WEAK MODIFIERS

Weak modifiers, permissible perhaps once in a manuscript for emphasis, can almost always be removed without changing the meaning of a sentence.

active	CUT
actively	CUT
actual	CUT
actually	CUT
any	CUT
available	CUT
both	CUT
careful	CUT
carefully	CUT
certain	CUT
certainly	CUT
comparative	CUT
comparatively	CUT
definite	CUT
definitely	CUT
effective	CUT
eminent	CUT
eminently	CUT
existing	CUT
fortunately	CUT
herself	CUT
himself	CUT
hopefully	CUT
in fact	CUT

in general	CUT
in particular	CUT
in the future	CUT
in the past	CUT
indeed	CUT
inevitably	CUT
itself	CUT
meaningful	CUT
meaningfully	CUT
namely	CUT
necessarily	CUT
needless to say	CUT
now	CUT
over time	CUT
overall	CUT
particular	CUT
particularly	CUT
per se	CUT
pretty	CUT
quite	CUT
rather	CUT
real	CUT
really	CUT
related	CUT
relatively	CUT
respectively	CUT
somewhat	CUT
specific	CUT
themselves	CUT
total	CUT
unfortunately	CUT
very	CUT

See the alphabetized entries in part II for more fat that can be trimmed from your sentences.

Chapter 2 **The Better Word**

Some words are better than others because they are correct, because they are right for the audience, because they illuminate an idea for the reader, or because they are preferred by most good writers most of the time. The more often you use the better word, the better your writing will seem to others.

Because there are so many possibilities, only a few examples are given under each heading to indicate what to watch. Note that you can avoid many problems simply by referring to the dictionary, which should be at hand when you are writing or editing.

WHAT TO PREFER

Prefer short words to long

accomplish	CHANGE TO	do
component	CHANGE TO	part
facilitate	TRY	ease, help, make easier
lengthy	CHANGE TO	long
utilization	TRY	use

Prefer concrete words to abstract

One red flag for abstraction is the suffix -*ion*. You should examine a noun ending in -*ion* to see whether it can be replaced by a concrete word.

motivation	TRY	drive
population	TRY	people
origination	TRY	source

Prefer specific words to general

facility	TRY	office building
lower-tract discomfort	TRY	diarrhea
natural fertilizer	TRY	cow dung
several	TRY	six
vehicle	TRY	car

Prefer everyday language to jargon

If you must use jargon, you should define it in parentheses on its first appearance.

adult literacy rate	TRY	percentage of people over fifteen who can read and write
discount rate	TRY	interest rate that the Fed charges banks for loans
morbidity and mortality	TRY	illness and death

Prefer singular nouns to plural

The distinction depends on whether you are writing about what makes up the aggregate or about the aggregate. If the second, use the singular and see how your writing improves.

benefits	TRY	benefit
costs	TRY	cost
elites	CHANGE TO	elite
expenditures	TRY	expenditure
moneys	CHANGE TO	money
pressures	TRY	pressure
revenues	TRY	revenue

But sometimes singular and plural nouns have different meanings, as with *saving* and *savings*.

See part II of this book for more plural nouns that can often be singular.

Prefer words to symbols, initials, and abbreviations

If you must use symbols, initials, and abbreviations, you should define them on their first appearance: for example, *the gross national product (GNP).*

etc.	CHANGE TO	and so on, and so forth
e.g.	CHANGE TO	for example
km	CHANGE TO	kilometers
%	CHANGE TO	percent
CDR	CHANGE TO	the crude death rate

Prefer American words and phrases to foreign

Foreign words and phrases include British idiosyncrasies (*as regards*). Recommendations for the treatment of Latin words, phrases, and abbreviations are drawn together at the end of part II.

a priori	TRY	deductive(ly), presumptive(ly)
as regards	TRY	on, for, about
ceteris paribus	TRY	other things being equal

Prefer familiar words to unfamiliar

defalcate	TRY	embezzle
defenestrate	TRY	throw out of a window
shrewdness of gorillas	TRY	family of gorillas

WHAT TO AVOID

Avoid contractions

don't	CHANGE TO	do not
here's	CHANGE TO	here is

Avoid ugly words ending in -wise and -ize

A few uses of the suffix *-wise* are legitimate: *clockwise, likewise, lengthwise,* and *otherwise.* Other uses border on excess, as do many uses of the suffix *-ize.*

electricitywise	CHANGE TO	about electricity
prioritize	CHANGE TO	set priorities for

Avoid overused phrases (and fad words and slang)

impact [as a verb]	CHANGE TO	affect, have an effect
interface	TRY	work together
bottom line	CHANGE TO	what this means
rationale	TRY	reason

WHAT ELSE TO WATCH

Watch prepositions

Many dictionaries, in their examples of usage, offer help on preferred prepositions. Part II of this book also has solutions to some of the more common mistakes.

conform with	CHANGE TO	conform to
correspond with [by letter]	COMPARE	correspond to [match, go with]
integrate into	CHANGE TO	integrate with
investigation into	CHANGE TO	investigation of

Watch seeming synonyms

There are two opposing tendencies in American usage. One is to attach one meaning to many words, making them synonyms. The other is to reserve one meaning for one word, another for another, keeping them distinct. The first tendency is a lapse into sloth, the second a desire for precision. Part II of this book gives more extensive advice on some of the more troublesome pairs and threesomes.

among [three or more]	COMPARE	between [two or two at a time]
contemptible [deserving scorn]	COMPARE	contemptuous [scornful]
imply [suggest]	COMPARE	infer [conclude]
masterful [strong-willed]	COMPARE	masterly [skillful]

Chapter 3   Pronoun References

Few things slow a reader down more than unclear pronoun references—signs of carelessness that quickly distract the reader from your meaning. The reader can usually divine what you mean, but only at a cost that need not be incurred. Here are two examples of the problem.

> *The main problem that people run into with pronouns*
> *arises from their...*

Does *their* refer to *people* or *pronouns?* The unfolding of the sentence may or may not give the answer.

> *The main problem that people run into with a pronoun*
> *is not tying it to its noun. It...*

Does *It* refer to *problem, pronoun, not tying it,* or *its noun?* Or is *It* indefinite? Again, the unfolding of the sentence may or may not give the answer.

That is why you should check each pronoun, whether personal, impersonal, relative, possessive, or substantive, to be sure that there is no question about which noun the pronoun stands for.

AMBIGUOUS PRONOUNS

If two or three nouns vie for a pronoun, the reference is almost certain to be ambiguous. The general solutions are to repeat the noun rather than use a pronoun or to eliminate the pretenders by changing their number.

The main problem that people run into with pronouns arises from their not being tied to a noun.	CHANGE TO	The main problem that people run into with pronouns arises from a pronoun's not being tied to a noun.
	OR	The main problem that a writer has with pronouns arises from their not being tied to a noun.

DISTANT PRONOUNS

Another big problem with pronouns is introducing them at some distance from their noun. That sets the pronoun adrift. It is solved by repeating the noun that the distant pronoun stands for.	CHANGE TO	Another big problem with pronouns is introducing them at some distance from their noun. That sets the pronoun adrift. The problem is solved by repeating the noun that the distant pronoun stands for.

Or get rid of the pronoun.

Many of the world's indigenous people take a view of nature that differs strikingly from conventional attitudes. They are estimated to number more than 250 million.	CHANGE TO	Many of the world's indigenous people—estimated to number more than 250 million—take a view of nature that differs strikingly from conventional attitudes.

PREMATURE PRONOUNS

If it is unambiguously tied to the noun it stands for, a pronoun...	CHANGE TO	If a pronoun is unambiguously tied to the noun it stands for, it...

If she wins an Oscar for her performance, Meryl Streep will be the...	CHANGE TO	If Meryl Streep wins an Oscar for her performance, she will be the...

VAGUE PRONOUNS

If *this, that, these,* and *those* are used not as adjectives, as in *This book is...*, but as pronouns, as in *This is...*, they often are vague. If there is any question, however fleeting, about what the pronoun refers to, restore the noun or create one.

Several countries have objected to recent decisions by the U.S. government to deplete its stockpile of tin. These will lodge a...	CHANGE TO	Several countries have objected to recent decisions by the U.S. government to deplete its stockpile of tin. These countries will lodge a...
The White House proposed an increase in aid to several Latin American countries. This has set off a barrage...	CHANGE TO	The White House proposed an increase in aid to several Latin American countries. This proposal has set off a barrage...

Note that such pronouns can stand alone if a verb separates them from what they stand for: *This is the reason that...*, *These are times that....*

ILLOGICAL PRONOUNS

Some pronouns illogically stand for a noun that is implicit, not stated.

Japan's exports of cars skyrocketed in the 1970s. The main reason is their skill in production.	CHANGE TO	Japan's exports of cars skyrocketed in the 1970s. The main reason is the skill of the Japanese in production.

Other pronouns illogically stand for nouns of a different number: that is, a singular pronoun stands for a plural noun, a plural pronoun for a singular noun.

Everyone has a right to the information they need to...	CHANGE TO	All people have a right to the information they need to...
	OR	Everyone has a right to the information he or she needs to...
Neither of the sloops have their crew aboard.	CHANGE TO	Neither of the sloops has its crew aboard.

Chapter 4 Order in the Sentence

The elements of pairs, series, and compound subjects and predicates usually appear as they come out of the writer's mind—haphazardly. Rearranging those elements from short to long and from simple to compound makes them easier for the reader to understand.

COUNT THE SYLLABLES

letters and arts	CHANGE TO	arts and letters
oranges and pears	CHANGE TO	pears and oranges

If the number of syllables is the same, count the letters.

COUNT THE WORDS

old-style politicians and reformers	CHANGE TO	reformers and old-style politicians
Raiders of the Lost Ark, Shane, and *Gone with the Wind*	CHANGE TO	*Shane, Gone with the Wind,* and *Raiders of the Lost Ark*
A Midsummer Night's Dream, Macbeth, and *King Lear*	CHANGE TO	*Macbeth, King Lear,* and *A Midsummer Night's Dream*
Washington, D.C., New York, and Miami	CHANGE TO	Miami, New York, and Washington, D.C.

PUT COMPOUND ELEMENTS LAST

liberty, the pursuit of happiness, and life	CHANGE TO	life, liberty, and the pursuit of happiness
He washed the glasses, dishes, and silverware, made the bed, and mopped the floor.	CHANGE TO	He made the bed, mopped the floor, and washed the dishes, glasses, and silverware.
The generally poor quality of education in public schools and crime are the main reasons.	CHANGE TO	Crime and the generally poor quality of education in public schools are the main reasons.
Korea picked up much of its technology from foreign suppliers of machinery, raw materials, and equipment or from foreign buyers.	CHANGE TO	Korea picked up much of its technology from foreign buyers or from foreign suppliers of equipment, machinery, and raw materials.

EXCEPTIONS

This simple way of injecting order into a disorderly sentence does not work all the time.

Use the obvious sequence or chronology

realism, classicism, and romanticism	CHANGE TO	classicism, romanticism, and realism
tea with lunch, dinner, and breakfast	CHANGE TO	tea with breakfast, lunch, and dinner

Avoid unintended modifiers

trade and money market rates	CHANGE TO	money market rates and trade
The Miser and *The Barber of Seville*	CHANGE TO	*The Barber of Seville* and *The Miser*

Use the familiar or explicit order

cream and peaches	CHANGE TO	peaches and cream
the bees and the birds	CHANGE TO	the birds and the bees
gold, myrrh, and frankincense	CHANGE TO	gold, frankincense, and myrrh

Earth, Venus, and Mercury are the three planets closest to the sun.

CHANGE TO

Mercury, Venus, and Earth are the three planets closest to the sun, in that order.

Chapter 5 Shorter Sentences

Long sentences—those of more than, say, twenty words—are often hard to read. Short sentences usually are not. Successions of long sentences are even harder to read. But broken up by the occasional short sentence, successions of long sentences are easier to read.

So it is that the appeal of every writer on style is: be brief! And so it is that the retort of every writer who lacks style is: it's not possible. Along with such corollaries as: complicated ideas call for complicated sentences. Or: short sentences lack style because they are choppy. The idea, however, is not to be brief all the time or even most of the time. The idea is to be brief unless you have a reason not to be. Even if you have a reason not to be brief, there are ways of handling a sentence that make it easier for your reader to follow what you are trying to say.

BREAK A LONG SENTENCE INTO
TWO OR MORE SENTENCES

The speaker, though paid $15,000 for an afternoon of talk, probably felt that the egg on his face was not worth it, and he must still be wondering how a person

CHANGE TO

The speaker, though paid $15,000 for an afternoon of talk, probably felt that the egg on his face was not worth it. He must still be wondering how a person once all

once all powerful could be subjected to such ignominy.		powerful could be subjected to such ignominy.
The immediate effects of the new economic policies have been to strike a bit of terror in the hearts of government workers, to plant smiles on the faces of the rich, and to put frowns on the faces of the poor, who have long benefited from the federal safety net.	TRY	The new economic policies have had three immediate effects. They have struck a bit of terror in the hearts of government workers. They have planted smiles on the faces of the rich. And they have put frowns on the faces of the poor, who have long benefited from the federal safety net.

CUT UNNECESSARY PHRASES AND CLAUSES

All subordinate clauses should be scrutinized to see whether they contribute to the thought. If not, they should be cut.

And they have put frowns on the faces of the poor, who have long benefited from the federal safety net.	CHANGE TO	And they have put frowns on the faces of the poor.
The problem, which remarkably few writers are aware of, is that of failing to set off a nonrestrictive clause by punctuation—whether by commas, dashes, or parentheses.	CHANGE TO	The problem is that of failing to set off a nonrestrictive clause by punctuation.

The same fate should befall the fat in a sentence.

The process of industrialization has served to help raise the GNP of many of the world's countries.	CHANGE TO	Industrialization has boosted the GNP of many countries.

JUDICIOUS REARRANGEMENT AND PUNCTUATION

Even if the length of a sentence stays much the same, judicious rearrangement and punctuation can give shape to otherwise amorphous elements.

Striking a bit of terror in the hearts of all taxpayers, planting smiles on the faces of congressional staffers, and putting frowns on the faces of tax shelter buffs, who have long benefited from loopholes and loose collection practices, have been the three immediate effects of the IRS's draconian policies for assessing penalties.	TRY	The IRS's draconian policies for assessing penalties have had three immediate effects: they have struck a bit of terror in the hearts of all taxpayers, planted smiles on the faces of congressional staffers, and put frowns on the faces of tax shelter buffs, who have long benefited from loopholes and loose collection practices.

Dashes should occasionally be used to set off parenthetical material that separates a subject from its verb.

Long sentences, which can be defined as those of more than, say, twenty words, often are hard to read.	CHANGE TO	Long sentences—those of more than, say, twenty words—often are hard to read.

Chapter 6   Dangling Constructions

Danglers are easy to avoid, generally by moving what they refer to immediately after them. The only difficult thing about danglers is learning to recognize them.

PARTICIPLES

The most notorious dangler is the participle that introduces a phrase at the beginning of a sentence.

DANGLING		ATTACHED
Walking to work after the blizzard, the sun's reflection on the snow almost blinded him.	CHANGE TO	While walking to work after the blizzard, he was almost blinded by the sun's reflection on the snow.
	OR	While he was walking to work after the blizzard, the sun's reflection on the snow almost blinded him.
Using official data and other information, these costs were allocated to specific activities.	CHANGE TO	Using official data and other information, we allocated these costs to specific activities.

	OR	Official data and other information were used to allocate these costs to specific activities.
Transposing the elements of the main clause, the dangling clause was tied to the subject by the author.	CHANGE TO	By transposing the elements of the main clause, the author tied the dangling clause to the subject.

In the foregoing examples on the left, the dangling constructions have the following unfortunate effects on meaning: *the sun's reflection* is *walking to work, these costs* are *using official data,* and *the dangling clause* is *transposing the elements.*

OTHER PARTS

DANGLING		ATTACHED
Before applying to graduate school, it is a good idea to master dangling gerunds.	CHANGE TO	Before you apply to graduate school, you should master dangling gerunds.
Once in graduate school, it is wise to be on the lookout for dangling elliptical clauses.	CHANGE TO	Once in graduate school, you would be wise to be on the lookout for dangling elliptical clauses.
	OR	Once you are in graduate school, you would be wise to be on the lookout for dangling elliptical clauses.
To get into graduate school, it is necessary to have mastered dangling infinitives.	CHANGE TO	To get into graduate school, you must have mastered dangling infinitives.

The red flag for a dangler is a sentence with an introductory word, phrase, or clause. To recognize the problem, see whether the introductory matter applies to what immediately follows it. To solve the problem, transpose the elements of the main clause. Or rewrite either the main clause or the introductory matter to attach properly what would otherwise be unattached or incorrectly attached.

Chapter 7 Abused Relatives

That, which, and *who* are often used as relative pronouns to introduce clauses that modify the nouns they follow. They are three of
the most useful, and used, words in the language. Being so useful,
they often are misused or overused.

Two definitions are in order. A *restrictive clause,* which is also
called a defining or limiting clause, defines a noun. A *nonrestrictive
clause,* also called an informing or commenting clause, adds information about a noun that has already been defined or does not need
definition. Here are some examples.

RESTRICTIVE CLAUSES	NONRESTRICTIVE CLAUSES
The book that (or which) I wrote in 1994 is about French politics.	My book on French politics, which I wrote in 1994, is about to be published.
The people who live next door are going to Hollywood.	The Moores, who live next door, are going to Hollywood.

A few comments should help clarify the differences between restrictive and nonrestrictive clauses even more. First, a restrictive clause
can be introduced by *that, which,* or *who;* a nonrestrictive clause by
which or *who.* Second, in the foregoing examples of restrictive
clauses, the reader does not know which *book* or which *people* are
being written about until the clause appears. The restrictive clause
is needed to define the *book* to distinguish it from other books and

to define the *people* to distinguish them from other people. Third, in the examples of nonrestrictive clauses, the reader already knows which *book* and which *Moores* are being written about when the clause appears. Note that nonrestrictive clauses can be cut without sacrificing the clarity of sentences and that restrictive clauses cannot.

PUNCTUATE NONRESTRICTIVE CLAUSES

Restrictive clauses never are set off by punctuation; nonrestrictive clauses always are.

INCORRECT		CORRECT
The main problem which remarkably few writers are aware of is that of failing to set off a nonrestrictive clause by punctuation—whether by commas, dashes, or parentheses.	CHANGE TO	The main problem, which remarkably few writers are aware of, is that of failing to set off a nonrestrictive clause by punctuation—whether by commas, dashes, or parentheses.

Writers who remember the first comma sometimes forget to put in the second.

WATCH CLAUSES THAT DO NOT FOLLOW
THE NOUN THEY MODIFY

Take this fragment as the problem: "The meaning of the sentence, which usually is obvious from...." How can you make it clear that the relative clause relates not to *sentence*, which it follows, but to *meaning*? Here are some solutions.

Make the object of the prepositional phrase plural and rely on verb number

The meaning of the sentence, which usually is obvious from...	TRY	The meaning of sentences, which usually is obvious from...

Repeat the noun before a relative clause

The meaning of the sentence, which usually is obvious from...	TRY	The meaning of the sentence, meaning which usually is obvious from...

Delete the intervening prepositional phrase

| The meaning of the sentence, which usually is obvious from... | TRY | The meaning, which usually is obvious from... |

Rewrite the sentence

| The meaning of the sentence, which usually is obvious from... | TRY | The meaning of sentences usually is obvious from... |

AVOID HOPSCOTCHING BETWEEN THAT AND WHICH

Many writers think a sentence is made more elegant by a restrictive clause introduced by *which*. But the usage that Fowler, Follett, Strunk and White, and many other arbiters of usage prefer is to use *that* for restrictive clauses, *which* for nonrestrictive. Such usage at least shows that the writer knows the difference between restrictive and nonrestrictive clauses.

ACCEPTABLE		PREFERRED
The book which I wrote in 1994 is about French politics.	CHANGE TO	The book that I wrote in 1994 is about French politics.

The use of *that* leaves no question about whether the clause is restrictive. And reserving *which* for nonrestrictive clauses leaves no question about which *which* clauses are to be punctuated. Note, however, the exception of restrictive clauses that begin with a preposition: *the manner in which she does things*. Note, too, that the exception can be circumvented by rewriting: *the way she does things*.

AVOID TOO MANY THAT'S, WHICH'S, AND WHO'S

A sentence or paragraph can have too many *that's*, as adjectives, conjunctions, relative pronouns, demonstrative pronouns, and other parts of speech. A sentence can also have too many *which*'s and *who*'s. Here are some common solutions.

Cut out "that is" and "that are" (and "who is" and "who are")

| Cars that are sold after January will not have a six-month warranty. | CHANGE TO | Cars sold after January will not have a six-month warranty. |

People who are living in glass houses should draw the blinds.		People living in glass houses should draw the blinds.

Cut out "which is" and "which are" (and "who is" and "who are")

A good solution, which is known as ellipsis, is to delete the *which* and the auxiliary verb—which is a solution that works best with *is* and *are*.	CHANGE TO	A good solution, known as ellipsis, is to delete the *which* and the auxiliary verb—a solution that works best with *is* and *are*.
The king, who is twenty-one today, will give up his throne.	CHANGE TO	The king, twenty-one today, will give up his throne.

Cut out unimportant nonrestrictive clauses

Decide whether a non-restrictive clause can be cut, which often is the fate it deserves.	TRY	Decide whether a non-restrictive clause can be cut.

Raise the nonrestrictive clause to a main or subordinate clause

Most nonrestrictive clauses are unimportant, but if they are not, raise them to a main or subordinate clause

Nonrestrictive clauses, which sometimes carry ideas important to the flow of argument, should sometimes be raised to the status of a main clause.	TRY	Nonrestrictive clauses sometimes carry ideas important to the flow of argument and should sometimes be raised to the status of a main clause.
	OR	If nonrestrictive clauses carry ideas important to the flow of argument, they should sometimes be raised to the status of a subordinate clause.

Chapter 8 The Active Voice

If the subject acts, the voice is active. If the subject is acted on, the voice is passive. The red flag for the passive voice is some variation of an auxiliary verb (*was, will be, have been, is being*), plus a past participle (*built, written, directed*), plus *by* if the actor is mentioned.

PASSIVE VOICE	ACTIVE VOICE
This book was written by me.	I wrote this book.
I was given an advance by the publisher.	The publisher gave me an advance.
It was planned that the book would be published (by them) in the fall of 1995.	W.W. Norton planned to publish the book in the fall of 1995.

Voice thus gives a choice. Too few writers take it, however, relying instead on the flaccid passive, which almost always takes more words. The active voice normally is shorter, livelier, and more direct—and so is usually preferred.

SWITCHING FROM PASSIVE VOICE TO ACTIVE

There are two usual ways of switching from the passive voice to the active. One is to transpose the subject and the object, cutting out the passive baggage in the bargain. The other is to give the sentence an active subject.

PASSIVE VOICE		ACTIVE VOICE

Transpose the subject and the object

| The bill will have to be approved by Congress. | CHANGE TO | Congress will have to approve the bill. |
| That book was written by Tom Wolfe. | CHANGE TO | Tom Wolfe wrote that book. |

Give the sentence an active subject

The book was written in 1994.	CHANGE TO	She wrote the book in 1994.
The tire will have to be changed.	CHANGE TO	You will have to change the tire.
It is expected...	CHANGE TO	We expect...
It is felt...	CHANGE TO	I feel...
It is thought...	CHANGE TO	Many people think...
It will be remembered that...	CHANGE TO	Remember that...

In making the impersonal personal, avoid the use of *one*, which is equally impersonal. If used more than once, it sounds overworked: *One wants to avoid having one's sentences sound overworked, doesn't one?*

WHEN TO USE THE PASSIVE VOICE

Some rule mongers would say that the passive voice should never be used (or would say that you should never use the passive voice). True, it generally is better to use the active voice because it is more direct and more concise. But the subject of the sentence should dictate voice. At issue is whether the subject of the sentence is the subject of the paragraph.

The passive has two justifiable uses, both of which turn on whether the actor is less important than what is acted on.

If the actor should be left out

| I manipulated the variables to see whether I could determine the direction of causation. | CHANGE TO | The variables were manipulated to determine the direction of causation. |

| The Department of Commerce of the United States government increased the incentives to encourage producers to export. | CHANGE TO | Incentives were increased to encourage producers to export. |

If what is acted on is the subject of the paragraph

| Jones, because of his experience in the Treasury, knows the budget. But the president might soon ask him to leave the Budget Office and take another position. | CHANGE TO | Jones, because of his experience in the Treasury, knows the budget. But he might soon be asked by the president to leave the Budget Office and take another position. |

Chapter 9 **Parallel Constructions**

Words and groups of words that do the same work are easier to read
if they are similar (parallel) in grammatical construction.

NOT PARALLEL		PARALLEL
Aides on Capitol Hill talk about running the country and the manipulation of constituents.	CHANGE TO	Aides on Capitol Hill talk about running the country and manipulating constituents.
Many Americans think that the media are attentive to insignificant details but that deeper issues are ignored.	CHANGE TO	Many Americans think that the media are attentive to insignificant details but not to deeper issues.

One red flag for the sameness of function is a coordinating conjunction—an *and, but, for,* or *nor*—which by definition joins words,
phrases, and clauses that have the same function or similar func-
tions. Another red flag is a pair of correlative conjunctions: *both—
and; either—or; whether—or; not only—but also.* The words and
groups of words that follow each part of the pair should be parallel
in construction. The construction of sentences presenting similar
facts or ideas should be parallel, too, as should any recurring
sentence parts.

PARALLELISM WITH COORDINATING CONJUNCTIONS

the mama bear, the papa bear, and their young cub	CHANGE TO	the mama bear, the papa bear, and the baby bear
Do not fold, put on a spindle, or mutilate.	CHANGE TO	Do not fold, spindle, or mutilate.
He entered gingerly, she with recklessness.	CHANGE TO	He entered gingerly, she recklessly.
the plumber's wrench, the carpenter's hammer, and the pen of the writer	CHANGE TO	the plumber's wrench, the carpenter's hammer, and the writer's pen
the good, the bad, and ugly	CHANGE TO	the good, the bad, and the ugly
schoolchildren and the parent	CHANGE TO	schoolchildren and parents
	OR	the schoolchild and the parent

PARALLELISM WITH CORRELATIVE CONJUNCTIONS

Neither a borrower, nor a person who borrows money be.	CHANGE TO	Neither a borrower, nor a lender be.
The sale of the land was opposed both by environmentalists and the tourism lobby.	CHANGE TO	The sale of the land was opposed both by environmentalists and by the tourism lobby.

Elements often are not parallel because one of the correlatives is out of place.

Solving the problem requires that you both recognize it and that you do something about it.	CHANGE TO	Solving the problem requires both that you recognize it and that you do something about it.

Chapter 10 **Consistency**

Consistency is one of the main things an editor looks for in a piece of writing, consistency in the style of spelling, of punctuation, and of writing numbers as words or figures. To be inconsistent is to be sloppy—say, by alternating between *travelled* and *traveled*, *10* and *ten*, or % and *percent*. So, above all, be consistent, even if eccentric. The idea is to pick one style and stick to it. The best way to keep track of the styles you have chosen is to write them on a style sheet (see chapter 11).

In the examples that follow, the styles consistently chosen in the right-hand column reflect the preferences of most editors today. In most of the examples, it would have been acceptable (but not preferable) to have consistently chosen the alternative style.

SPELLING

Follow the style of spelling and the first entries of different acceptable spellings in the tenth edition of *Merriam-Webster's Collegiate Dictionary*, the dictionary most editors use.

INCONSISTENT   CONSISTENT

Words with two or more acceptable spellings

| *sizable* on one page and *sizeable* on the next | CHANGE TO | *sizable* on one page and *sizable* on the next |

traveling on one page and *travelling* on the next	CHANGE TO	*traveling* on one page and *traveling* on the next

Different words serving one function

nonetheless on one page and *nevertheless, none the less,* or *never the less* on the next	CHANGE TO	nonetheless on one page and *nonetheless* on the next
Second, on one page and *Secondly,* on the next	CHANGE TO	*Second,* on one page and *Second,* on the next

Latin plurals

formulas on one page and *formulae* on the next	CHANGE TO	*formulas* on one page and *formulas* on the next

OPEN, SOLID, AND HYPHENATED TERMS

Consult a dictionary to find out the accepted spelling of compound nouns, whether open *(field worker)*, solid *(fieldworker)*, or hyphenated *(field-worker)*. Hyphenate compound adjectives *(long-term gains)*, unless they are recognizable as paired adjectives that usually modify the noun they are in front of *(current account deficit)*. Run prefixes solid (without a hyphen), unless such curiosities as *crosssectional* are the result, or unless the prefix is attached to a compound word *(non-oil-exporting)* or a capitalized word *(non-British)*.

INCONSISTENT		CONSISTENT

Prefixes

antismoking on one page and *anti-smoking* on the next	CHANGE TO	*antismoking* on one page and *antismoking* on the next
nonviolent on one page and *non-violent* on the next	CHANGE TO	*nonviolent* on one page and *nonviolent* on the next

Compound nouns

cost-effectiveness on one page and *cost effectiveness* on the next	CHANGE TO	*cost-effectiveness* on one page and *cost-effectiveness* on the next
decision making on one page and *decision-making* on the next	CHANGE TO	*decision making* on one page and *decision making* on the next

Compound adjectives

low-income groups on one page and *low income groups* on the next	CHANGE TO	*low-income groups* on one page and *low-income groups* on the next
short-term gains on one page and *short term gains* on the next	CHANGE TO	*short-term gains* on one page and *short-term gains* on the next

CAPITALS

If you have a choice of using a capital or a small letter, use the small letter. Use capitals only when you must, never for emphasis.

INCONSISTENT		CONSISTENT
in figure 2 on one page and *in Figure 2* on the next	CHANGE TO	*in figure 2* on one page and *in figure 2* on the next
the president on one page and *the President* on the next	CHANGE TO	*the president* on one page and *the president* on the next
the project on one page and *the Project* on the next	CHANGE TO	*the project* on one page and *the project* on the next

SYMBOLS AND ABBREVIATIONS

The preferred practice is to avoid symbols and abbreviations. An exception is to use symbols for currencies in numerals (*$400*).

INCONSISTENT		CONSISTENT
Symbols		
percent on one page and % on the next	CHANGE TO	*percent* on one page and *percent* on the next
ten degrees on one page and *10°* on the next	CHANGE TO	*ten degrees* on one page and *ten degrees* on the next
Abbreviations of unit		
kilometers on one page and *km* on the next	CHANGE TO	*kilometers* on one page and *kilometers* on the next

square feet on one page and *sq ft* on the next	CHANGE TO	*square feet* on one page and *square feet* on the next

Abbreviations of Latin terms

and so on on one page and *etc.* on the next	CHANGE TO	*and so on* on one page and *and so on* on the next
that is on one page and *i.e.* on the next	CHANGE TO	*that is* on one page and *that is* on the next

Other abbreviations

months on one page and *mos* on the next	CHANGE TO	*months* on one page and *months* on the next

INITIALS

The main problem with initials is that they are difficult to under-stand. If you must use them, spell the words they represent on their first appearance, followed by the initials in parentheses [*the gross national product (GNP)*], and then use initials. Initials read one by one are preceded by an article (*the GNP*); those read as a word are not (*OPEC*).

INCONSISTENT		CONSISTENT
by OPEC on one page and *by the OPEC* on the next	CHANGE TO	*by OPEC* on one page and *by OPEC* on the next
of the GNP on one page and *of GNP* on the next	CHANGE TO	*of the GNP* on one page and *of the GNP* on the next
the United States on one page and *the U.S.* on the next	CHANGE TO	*the United States* on one page and *the United States* on the next

NUMBERS

One style is to use words for single-digit numbers and to use numer-als for all others; another is to use words for single-digit and dou-ble-digit numbers and to use numerals for all others. Percentages should nonetheless be written as numerals (*2 percent*); large rough numbers as words (*a million*); large precise numbers as a combination of numerals and words (*1.3 billion*). There naturally are other views. Some editors recommend the use of figures all the time; others, the use of words, even for *three million four hundred ninety thousand dollars*. Whatever the system you adopt, be consistent.

INCONSISTENT		CONSISTENT
two cars on one page and 2 *cars* on the next	CHANGE TO	*two cars* on one page and *two cars* on the next
the first on one page and *the 1st* on the next	CHANGE TO	*the first* on one page and *the first* on the next
eleven o'clock on one page and 11 *o'clock* on the next	CHANGE TO	*eleven o'clock* on one page and *eleven o'clock* on the next
1950s on one page and *50's, 1950's, fifties, Fifties, nineteen fifties,* or *Nineteen Fifties* on the next	CHANGE TO	*1950s* on one page and *1950s* on the next
0.5 on one page and *.5* on the next	CHANGE TO	*0.5* on one page and *0.5* on the next
1994-95 on one page and *1994-1995* on the next	CHANGE TO	*1994-95* on one page and *1994-95* on the next
two-thirds on one page and 2/3 on the next	CHANGE TO	*two-thirds* on one page and *two-thirds* on the next

PUNCTUATION

The main incidents of inconsistency in punctuation are with series, with quotation marks, and with introductory phrases.

INCONSISTENT		CONSISTENT
the apples, oranges, and pears on one page and *the apples, oranges and pears* on the next	CHANGE TO	*the apples, oranges, and pears* on one page and *the apples, oranges, and pears* on the next
France, Germany, and Switzerland on one page and *France, Germany and Switzerland* on the next	CHANGE TO	*France, Germany, and Switzerland* on one page and *France, Germany, and Switzerland* on the next

*the "health gap." * on one page and *the "health gap".* on the next	CHANGE TO	*the "health gap." * on one page and *the "health gap."* on the next
In 1990 the Russians... on one page and *In 1990, the Russians...* on the next	CHANGE TO	*In 1990 the Russians...* on one page and *In 1990 the Russians...* on the next
After the war they... on one page and *After the war, they...* on the next	CHANGE TO	*After the war they...* on one page and *After the war they...* on the next

Chapter *11*   **Basic Tools**

Two important contributors to good writing are to continue learning and to find answers to questions. The two go hand in hand, and to help you do them you need some basic tools.

Dictionary

Keep a dictionary within reach when you are writing or editing. Many editors use the tenth edition of *Merriam-Webster's Collegiate Dictionary* (Springfield, Mass.: Merriam-Webster, Inc., 1994).

- Use it to find out what words mean and to confirm that words mean what you think they mean.
- Use it to find out the preferred spelling of a word.
- Use it to see a word in context: *dialectical*, a ~ philosopher.
- Use it to find out what preposition to use: *methodical*, ~ in his daily routine.
- Use it to see how seeming synonyms can be differentiated. For example, see the entry for *masterful* in *Merriam-Webster's Dictionary* to see how that word can be differentiated from *domineering, imperious, peremptory,* and *imperative.*

A dictionary also helps in finding the accepted spelling of the names of people and places. And many dictionaries have a section on style and punctuation (*Merriam-Webster's Dictionary*, pp. 1535-57).

Style sheet

To be consistent in spelling, punctuation, hyphenation, capitalization, and writing numbers in words or numerals, keep a style sheet. Indispensable for writing by one person, and imperative for writing by more than one person, a style sheet is a simple tool that can save time and avoid confusion (see the sample on page 42). It is made by drawing a few lines on a sheet of paper and writing groups of initials in each box. Each time you write or see a word that has more than one acceptable style, write it in the appropriate box; for example, write *decision making* in the ABCD box, *traveling* in the QRST box. When you run into these words elsewhere, you can check the style against the style sheet (rather than having to flip through all the pages to see how you spelled them the first time). For long pieces it often helps to keep a style sheet for each of the common areas of inconsistency: one for spelling (especially that of names and terms), one for hyphens, one for capitals, one for numbers, and one for initials.

Checklist

You should check the use and usefulness of each word, phrase, sentence, paragraph, and section. If you do not have time for such a task, at least check a few basic things.

- Check all spelling, hyphens, capitals, numbers, and important names and terms against your style sheet.

- Make a contents page to identify problems of organization and to help your readers.

- Underline and try to rectify long sentences, awkward sentences, passive verbs, and constructions that should be parallel but are not.

- Check that subjects and verbs agree in number.

- Check that all *who* and *which* clauses are correctly punctuated.

- Check that all introductory clauses beginning with an *-ing* word relate to what immediately follows.

- Check that pairs, series, and compound subjects and predicates are arranged from short to long, from simple to compound.

- Cut what is of little use.

- Proofread everything you send out. A list of proofreader's marks is under *proofreader* in *Merriam-Webster's Dictionary.*

SAMPLE STYLE SHEET

ABCD	EFGH
antismoking	(the) executive director
busing	formulas (plural)
benefited	figure 1
channeling	
cooperate	
cost-effectiveness	
decision making	

IJKL	MNOP
	midproject
	multidisciplinary
	nonviolent
	percent
	(the) project

QRST	UVWXYZ
sizable	
short-term (adj.)	
table 1	
traveling	
tradable	

NUMBERS		INITIALS, NAMES, AND IMPORTANT TERMS
1980s	2 million	EU = European Union
mid-1970s	1,215	GDP = gross domestic product
1980-81	first	
$400	eleven o'clock	
two cars	three-quarters	
2 percent		
2 percentage		
points		

Part II **WHAT EDITORS CUT,
CHANGE, AND COMPARE**

The recommendations in this part are just that: recommendations. But nine times out of ten, the recommendations will give you a sentence that is more clear, more concise, and the product of a careful writer. The recommendations do not always work, but if they do not, they may point to other problems that call for another try at writing the sentence. The idea underlying the brevity and precision proposed here is to throw attention on the words and phrases that deserve attention in a sentence.

The recommendations CUT and CHANGE TO indicate cuts and changes that almost always are preferred because they trim fat or because they avoid words and phrases that are overused, are long when they could be short, or depart from current usage. The recommendations TRY and TRY TO CUT indicate changes and cuts that you should consider because they are preferred in many instances, but not all. The recommendation COMPARE indicates a choice to be made depending on the meaning and context. In phrases that are alphabetically placed according to words other than the first, the preceding word or words are enclosed by parentheses: for example, *(for the) purpose of* is placed under *p*.

The brackets after an entry enclose information either to help define a word or to identify what part of speech a word is: for example, *adverse [bad, unfavorable]* and *accord [the verb]*. Recommendations for the treatment of Latin words, phrases, and abbreviations are drawn together at the end.

A | A | A

| a | COMPARE | an |

Before *h*, *a* is preferred if the *h* is voiced, as in *a hotel*,
and *an* if it is not, as in *an hour*.

| a, an [general] | COMPARE | the [particular] |

The article *a* (*an*) goes before an indefinite one
of a class, as in *a book*; the article *the* before a definite
one of a class, as in *the book*.
No article is used for all of a class, as in *books*;
but *the* is used for some of a class, as in *the books of X*.
A tendency, not to be indulged, is to drop *the* before
singular constructions followed by a prepositional
phrase: *practice of family planning* should be
the practice of family planning.

a lot of	CHANGE TO	much, many
(in) abeyance	CHANGE TO	held up
absolutely	CUT	
access [the verb]	TRY	get, find, get into
accomplish	TRY	do
accord [the verb]	TRY	give
(in) accordance with	TRY	by, under, in accord with
accordingly	TRY TO CUT OR TRY	so, therefore
(take into) account	COMPARE	take account of
account for	TRY	explain, make up
(on) account of	CHANGE TO	caused by, because of
achieve	TRY	do, get, reach
achieve (reductions)	CHANGE TO	reduce
acquaint	CHANGE TO	tell, inform
acquiesce with	CHANGE TO	acquiesce to
acquire	TRY	get
across the board	TRY	all
act to	CUT	
action	TRY	act
(take) action	CHANGE TO	act
active(ly)	CUT	
actual(ly)	CUT	

acute	TRY TO CUT	
(in) addition	TRY	and, also
(in) addition to	TRY	besides, on top of, other than, over and above
additional	CHANGE TO	added, new, more
additionally	CHANGE TO	moreover, and, also
adjacent to	CHANGE TO	near, next to, close to
administrate	CHANGE TO	administer
admit of [leave possibility for]	COMPARE	admit
admit to (something)	CHANGE TO	admit (something)
admittance [permission for access to a physical space]	COMPARE	admission [all other uses]
adventuresome	CHANGE TO	adventurous
adverse [bad, unfavorable]	COMPARE	averse [opposed, disinclined]
advert to	CHANGE TO	refer to
advise	TRY	tell, inform
advocate that	CHANGE TO	advocate
affect [the verb: influence]	COMPARE	effect [the verb: bring about], effect [the noun: result]
affirmative	TRY	yes
afford [the verb]	CHANGE TO	give
(the) aforementioned ~	CHANGE TO	that ~, those ~s
against	TRY	compared with
aggravate [the noun]	CHANGE TO	annoy, make worse
aggregate	TRY	whole, entire
agree on, to, with	CHANGE TO	agree on a course of action, agree to terms proposed, agree with an adversary
albeit	CHANGE TO	though, although
all [the adjective]	TRY TO CUT	
all of	CHANGE TO	all
all together [collectively]	COMPARE	altogether [completely]
alleged	TRY TO CUT	
allows for	CHANGE TO	allows
allude [refer indirectly]	COMPARE	refer [directly]

allusion [indirect reference]	COMPARE	reference [direct]
allusion [indirect reference]	COMPARE	delusion [deception of belief], illusion [visual deception or false perception]
alongside of	CHANGE TO	alongside
already has been	TRY	has been
alright [not a word]	CHANGE TO	all right
Also,...	CHANGE TO	And..., ...also...

Most editors would change *Also, I fell ill* to
And I fell ill or *I also fell ill.*

(and) also	CHANGE TO	and
alter(ation)	CHANGE TO	change
alternate(ly) [by turns]	COMPARE	alternative(ly) [of choice]
alternative [the adjective]	CHANGE TO	other, different

Let *alternative* stand as an adjective if it refers to
a choice between two or more things.

alternative [the noun]	TRY	method, choice
alternative(ly) [of choice]	COMPARE	alternate(ly) [by turns]
alternatively	TRY	or
although	TRY	but, though
altogether [completely]	COMPARE	all together [collectively]
ameliorate	CHANGE TO	improve
amidst	CHANGE TO	amid
among [three or more]	COMPARE	between [two or two at a time]

The conventional practice is to reserve *between* for two,
among for three or more.
Thus: *The winnings were divided between the two of them*
or *among the three of them.*
But *between* is used for three or more if what is
described applies to two at a time.
Thus: *Trade between western nations.*

among others	TRY TO CUT	
amongst	CHANGE TO	among

(the) amount of ~	CHANGE TO	the ~
an historical	CHANGE TO	a historical
analogous	CHANGE TO	similar
and also	TRY	and
~ and/or ~	CHANGE TO	~ and ~, ~ or ~
anterior	CHANGE TO	before
anticipate that	TRY	expect that
antipathy for	CHANGE TO	antipathy to or toward
any	TRY TO CUT	
apart from	TRY	except for
(it is) apparent that	CUT	
(it) appears that	CUT	
appears to be	COMPARE	is
append	CHANGE TO	add
apprise	CHANGE TO	tell, inform
approach [the noun]	TRY	way, method
approbation [praise for an act]	COMPARE	approval [praise for general behavior]
appropriate [the adjective]	TRY	right, proper
approval [praise for general behavior]	COMPARE	approbation [praise for an act]
approximately	COMPARE	about, roughly

If something has been mathematically approximated,
use *approximately*. If a precise figure is being rounded
or if an imprecise figure is being glossed,
use *about* or *roughly*.

are	COMPARE	is

Such pronouns as *each, none, either,* and *neither*
are singular and call for a singular verb:
each of them is; none of them is;
either of the two is; neither of the two is.
Some writers and editors use a plural verb if the sense
of the pronoun is collective, or if there is an
intervening prepositional phrase with a plural object,
as in *neither of them are coming.*
It is recommended here that you use the singular verb
unless you have a good reason for using the plural.
Whatever your choice, be consistent.

are ~ing   TRY   ~

> The construction of *are* plus a present participle
> is often used unnecessarily:
> *The farmers are producing corn and beans*
> is often written when the meaning is
> *The farmers produce corn and beans.*

are used to	CUT	
(in the) area of ~	TRY	in ~
arguable	CHANGE TO	can be argued that, can be questioned whether
arguably	CUT	
arising from the fact that	CHANGE TO	because
around (20 percent)	CHANGE TO	about (20 percent)
around the world	TRY	globally
As	CHANGE TO	If, When, Since, Because
as	COMPARE	like

> The use of *as* and *like* is muddied by misuse in speech,
> misuse that should not invade writing.
> A simple distinction covering most cases is to reserve
> *as* for constructions that have a verb,
> *like* for those that do not.
> Thus: *She acts like a child; she acts as a child would act.*
> This distinction does not apply to constructions
> with a verb in a modifying clause:
> *The children in the community, like*
> *children living anywhere in the Third World,...*

(such) as   COMPARE   like

> In introducing examples, use *such as* rather than *like:*
> *Some countries, such as Poland (not: like Poland), are*
> *overextended in their external debt.*
> Reserve *like* for likenesses: *Brazil, like Poland, may be*
> *overextended in its external debt.*

as a consequence of	TRY	because
as a result of	CUT OR TRY	so, with, from, because of
as a way to	TRY	to
as a whole	TRY	entire

as can be seen	CUT	
as follow	CHANGE TO	as follows
as if	COMPARE	like

> Reserve *as if* for constructions that can stand
> as sentences, *like* for those that cannot.
> Thus: *It looks as if I may be fired;*
> *it looks like another month of heavy layoffs.*

as long as	COMPARE	so long as

> Purists reserve *as long as* for positive
> constructions, *so long as* for negative:
> *As long as you succeed*
> but *So long as you do not fail.*

as long as	TRY	if
as noted earlier	TRY TO CUT	
as of	CHANGE TO	starting, beginning
as per	CHANGE TO	on, for, about, further to, in accord with
as regards	CHANGE TO	on, for, about
(~) as such	CHANGE TO	~
as to	TRY TO CUT OR CHANGE TO	in, of, on, for, about
as to whether (or why, how, what, who)	CHANGE TO	whether (or why, how, what, who)
as well as	TRY	and, also
assist(ance)	TRY	help
associated with	TRY	of
(in) association with	CHANGE TO	with
assuming that	TRY	if
assure [someone that]	COMPARE	ensure [that], insure [something]
assuredly	CUT	
at constant (or current) prices	CHANGE TO	in constant (or current) prices
at that time	CUT	
at the end of	TRY	after
at the same time	CUT OR TRY	and, while
at this time	CUT	
attain	TRY	get or gain

attempt	TRY	try
autarchy [sovereignty]	COMPARE	autarky [self-sufficiency]
author [as a verb]	CHANGE TO	write
available [a word to avoid]	TRY TO CUT	
averse [opposed, disinclined	COMPARE	adverse [bad, unfavorable]

B   B   B

(date, refer, or return) back	TRY	date (or refer or return)
(the) balance	TRY	the rest, remainder
barring	TRY	without, except for
based on	CHANGE TO	by, for, from, because of
Based on ~ , ...	TRY	~ shows that
basically	CUT	
(on an annual) basis	CHANGE TO	yearly, annually, once a year
(on a regular) basis	CHANGE TO	regularly
(on a year-to-year) basis	CHANGE TO	year to year
(on the) basis of	CHANGE TO	by, on, for, from, because of
be [the subjunctive verb]	TRY	is, are, should be
be helpful	CHANGE TO	help
(is) because	CHANGE TO	is that, is caused by, is attributable to
(the reason is) because	CHANGE TO	the reason is that
begin	TRY	start
(the issue) being addressed is	CHANGE TO	the issue is
believe [for convictions]	COMPARE	feel [for emotions], think [for speculations]
benefits	TRY	benefit
beside [next to]	COMPARE	besides [except, in addition]
bestow	TRY	give
between [two or two at a time]	COMPARE	among [three or more]

See the comments under *among*.

between 1980–90	CHANGE TO	during 1980–90, between 1980 and 1990
biannually	CHANGE TO	every two years, twice a year
bimonthly	CHANGE TO	every two months, twice a month
biweekly	CHANGE TO	every two weeks, twice a week
bored with	CHANGE TO	bored by
both	TRY TO CUT OR TRY	they, the two
both of them are	CHANGE TO	they are
but	COMPARE	and

But is often used when and would be better
or even correct, especially in joining independent
clauses that are not contradictory or exceptional.
A good practice is to try replacing but by and.

but rather	CHANGE TO	but
by itself	CHANGE TO	alone
by means of	CHANGE TO	by
by no means	TRY	not
(rose or fell) by 2 percent	CHANGE TO	rose (or fell) 2 percent
by virtue of	CHANGE TO	by
by way of ~ing	CHANGE TO	to ~

C   C   C

can [ability]	COMPARE	may [permission], might [possibility]
cannot help not	CHANGE TO	can only
capability	TRY	ability
(is) capable of	CHANGE TO	can
capacity	COMPARE	ability, capability

Reserve capacity for volumes and amounts,
ability and capability for what can be done.
Thus: The capacity of the container is ten gallons.
The capacity of the machine is 1,000 units a day.
The machine has the ability to produce several products.
People have abilities, not capacities.

capital [of column or country]	COMPARE	Capitol [building]
careful(ly)	TRY TO CUT	
case [a word to avoid]	TRY TO CUT	

Misused, overused, and otherwise abused,
the word *case* has at least six acceptable uses:
*a case of yellow fever, you have no case, in case of need, a
case of burglary, a law case, the case of Quiller-Couch.*
The examples here are borrowed from Gowers, who
borrowed them from Fowler.
A seventh acceptable use is the main use:
a case of beer. But note in the following lines
how many constructions that use
case can be shortened.

(in that) case	TRY	then
case in point	CUT OR TRY	example
(in the) case of	TRY TO CUT OR TRY	by, in, of, for
(than is the) case with ~	CHANGE TO	than with ~
(in) cases in which	CHANGE TO	if, when
category	TRY	class, group
cater for	CHANGE TO	cater to
cease	TRY	stop
ceiling	TRY	limit, maximum
center around	CHANGE TO	center on
(a) certain ~	TRY	a ~
certainly	CUT	
(is of a ~) character	CHANGE TO	is ~

For example: *The house is of a rustic character*
should be *The house is rustic.*

(~ in) character	CHANGE TO	~

For example: *The food is mild in character*
should be *The food is mild.*

(~ of this) character	CHANGE TO	~ such as, ~ like this
clearly	CUT	
coauthor [the verb]	CHANGE TO	write with
cognizant	CHANGE TO	aware

combines ~ with ~	TRY	combines ~ and ~
commence	CHANGE TO	start, begin
common [of many]	COMPARE	mutual [reciprocated]
comparable to	TRY	the same as
comparatively	TRY TO CUT	
compare to [liken]	COMPARE	compare with [set side by side]
(in) comparison to	CHANGE TO	in comparison with
compensate (compensation)	TRY	pay, reward
compensate by	TRY	offset
complete	TRY	finish
completely	TRY TO CUT	
component	CHANGE TO	part
compose [constitute, make up]	COMPARE	consist of [comprise, is made up of]

Accepted usage is this: *the team is made up of*
(or *consists of* or *comprises*) *nine players;*
nine players make up (or *compose* or *constitute*) *the team.*
Constitute and *comprise* should be reserved for
scholarly writing.

comprehensive	TRY	overall
comprise [consist of, is made up of]	COMPARE	constitute [compose, make up]

See the comments under *compose.*

comprise [all parts]	COMPARE	include [some parts]
conceal	TRY	hide
(the) concept of ~	CHANGE TO	~
(so far as ~ is) concerned	CHANGE TO	for ~
(where ~ is) concerned	CHANGE TO	for ~
(the ~) concerned are	CHANGE TO	the ~ are
concerning	CHANGE TO	at, of, on, for, about
(the) conclusions reached	CHANGE TO	the conclusions
confident of	CHANGE TO	sure of, sure that
conform with	CHANGE TO	conform to
(in this) connection	CHANGE TO	about
(in) connection with	CHANGE TO	on, for, about

connote [signify attributes of a word]	COMPARE	denote [define meaning of a word]

The word *table* usually *denotes* a raised surface on legs;
it can *connote* dining.

conscious (efforts)	CHANGE TO	efforts
(general) consensus	CHANGE TO	consensus
consensus of opinion	CHANGE TO	consensus
consequence	TRY	result, effect
consequently	TRY	so, therefore
consider	TRY	explore, examine, think about
considerable	CUT OR TRY	many, long
considerably (greater)	TRY	far greater
(take into) consideration	CHANGE TO	consider
consist of [is made up of]	COMPARE	compose [make up]

See the comments under *compose.*

consistently	TRY TO CUT	
constant 1975 prices	CHANGE TO	1975 prices
(at) constant prices	CHANGE TO	in constant prices
constitute [compose, make up]	COMPARE	comprise [consist of, is made up of]

See the comments under *compose.*

constitute	TRY	be, are, make up
constructive(ly)	TRY TO CUT	
contained	TRY	had
contained in	TRY	in
contemptible [deserving scorn]	COMPARE	contemptuous [scornful]
contemptuous [scornful]	COMPARE	contemptible [deserving scorn]
contend for, with, against	CHANGE TO	contend for ideals, contend with neighbors, contend against bad weather
contiguous with	CHANGE TO	contiguous to
continual [recurring with interruptions]	COMPARE	continuous [occurring without interruption]

The flow of water is *continuous;*
the dripping of water is *continual.*

continuous [occurring without interruption]	COMPARE	continual [recurring with interruptions]
(on the) contrary	TRY	no
(to the) contrary	TRY	not so
(a) contrast of X and Y	CHANGE TO	a contrast between X and Y
contrast to [the verb]	CHANGE TO	contrast with
(in) contrast with	CHANGE TO	unlike, in contrast to
(a) contrast with Y	CHANGE TO	a contrast to Y
contribute to	TRY	add to
converse	COMPARE	obverse, reverse

Consider the statement: *All authors are good writers.*
The *converse* is: *Some good writers are authors.*
The *obverse* is: *No authors are bad writers.*
The *converse* and *obverse* are each the *reverse*
of the first statement.

convince [someone of, that]	COMPARE	persuade [someone of, to, that]

There is much overlap except before *to,* where only
persuade will do. You can *persuade* or *convince* someone
of the wisdom *of* a policy; you can *persuade* or *convince*
someone *that* a policy is wise; you can *persuade*
(but not *convince*) someone *to* adopt a policy.

cooperate together with	CHANGE TO	cooperate with
(with the) cooperation of	TRY	with the help of
correspond with [by letter]	COMPARE	correspond to [match, go with]
costs [the noun]	TRY	cost
counteract	TRY	counter
counteracting	TRY	offsetting, countering
(of) course	CUT	
(in the) course of	TRY	in, during
credence [trust, belief]	COMPARE	credibility [of being believable], credulity [of readiness to believe]

credible [believable]	COMPARE	creditable [deserving credit], credulous [willing to believe]
critical	TRY TO CUT	
crucial	TRY TO CUT	
culminate with	CHANGE TO	culminate in
cultivatable	CHANGE TO	cultivable
cum	CHANGE TO	and, with
(at) current prices	CHANGE TO	in current prices
currently	CUT OR CHANGE TO	now

D	**D**	**D**
data is	CHANGE TO	data are
date back to	CHANGE TO	began, date to
(a good, a great) deal of	TRY	much
decide about this	CHANGE TO	decide this
decidedly	CUT	
(make a) decision	CHANGE TO	decide
decisions made by	CHANGE TO	decisions by
decrease [the noun or intransitive verb]	CHANGE TO	drop, fall
decrease [the transitive verb]	TRY	cut, reduce, shorten
defective [of quality]	COMPARE	deficient [of quantity]
deficient [of quantity]	COMPARE	defective [of quality]
definite(ly)	TRY TO CUT	
definitive [final, conclusive]	COMPARE	definite [decided, explicit]
(the) degree of ~	CHANGE TO	the ~
delusion [deception of belief]	COMPARE	allusion [indirect reference], illusion [visual deception or false perception]
demonstrate	TRY	show
denote [define meaning]	COMPARE	connote [signify attributes of a word]

See the comments under *connote.*

depend(ing) upon	CHANGE TO	depend(ing) on
(examine in) depth	CHANGE TO	examine
desiderata	CHANGE TO	desired things
(program) designed to	CHANGE TO	program that
desire	TRY	want, wish
(is) desirous of	CHANGE TO	wants
desist	CHANGE TO	stop
despite the fact that	CHANGE TO	although
determine	TRY	test, know, cause, study, decide, find out
devoid of	CHANGE TO	without
did [as intensifier]	TRY TO CUT	

For example: *did provide* usually should be *provided*.

differ from, with, over, about	CHANGE TO	differ from something, differ with neighbors over or about the election
differ(ent) than	CHANGE TO	differ(ent) from
(in three) different ways	CHANGE TO	in three ways
differential [for math or car]	COMPARE	difference, different [for everything else]
dilemma	COMPARE	difficulty

The word *dilemma* means two horns,
so it is illogical to say *horns of a dilemma*.
The word should be used for a choice between
two unsatisfactory things or courses of action.

dimension	CUT OR TRY	feature
disassociate	CHANGE TO	dissociate
discreet [circumspect]	COMPARE	discrete [separate]
discrepancy	TRY	difference
discrete [separate]	COMPARE	discreet [circumspect]
disinterested [impartial]	COMPARE	uninterested [not interested]
dispatch	TRY	send, send off
dissent with	CHANGE TO	dissent from
distinct [clear]	COMPARE	distinctive [individual]
distinctive [individual]	COMPARE	distinct [clear]
diverge(nt)	TRY	differ(ent)

do [as intensifier]	TRY TO CUT	

See the comments under *did.*

donate	TRY	give
double	COMPARE	twice

Usage now seems to be to reserve *double* for the verb
and *twice* for the noun, as in:
I'll double what I give you;
I'll give you twice that amount.

doubt if	TRY	doubt that
doubtless(ly)	CUT	
draw a comparison between	CHANGE TO	compare
due to	TRY	caused by, because of
due to the fact that	CHANGE TO	because
dwell	CHANGE TO	live
dynamic	CUT	
dynamics	TRY	processes

E	E	E
each and every	CHANGE TO	each, every
each of them are	CHANGE TO	each of them is
effect [the verb: bring about]	COMPARE	affect [the verb: influence], effect [the noun: result]
(have an) effect	CHANGE TO	affect
(may have the) effect of increasing	CHANGE TO	may increase
effective(ly)	TRY TO CUT	
effectuate	CHANGE TO	carry out, put into effect
(in an) effort to	CHANGE TO	to
e.g. [*exempli gratia* = by way of example]	CHANGE TO	say, such as, for example
e.g. [for example]	COMPARE	i.e. [that is]
either A, B, or C	CHANGE TO	A, B, or C
either of the three	CHANGE TO	any of the three
either of the two are	CHANGE TO	either of the two is

elapse	CHANGE TO	pass
elect [when voting]	COMPARE	choose [when choosing]
electric	COMPARE	electrical, electronic

Keep these adjectives straight by keeping in mind
that *electric* and *electrical* relate to electricity,
the shorter word being preferred unless it is confusing,
and that *electronic* relates to electrons
moving not in wires but in tubes and transistors. So:
electric clock, electrical knowledge, and *electronic watch.*

element	TRY	part
eliminate	TRY	end, stop, cut out
elites	CHANGE TO	elite
elucidate	CHANGE TO	explain
elusive [for that sought]	COMPARE	illusory [for that gained]
emerging	TRY	new
emigrate to	CHANGE TO	migrate to, emigrate from
eminently	CUT	
emphasize	TRY	stress
empirically	CUT	
employ	TRY	use
employment	TRY	jobs, work
encounter	TRY	meet, run into
encourage	TRY	urge
(at the) end of	TRY	after
end product	CHANGE TO	product
end result	CHANGE TO	result
endeavor [the noun and verb]	CHANGE TO	try, attempt
engage in	CHANGE TO	do, work on
enhance [heighten or increase]	TRY	make bigger, greater, or larger
enormity [outrageousness]	COMPARE	enormousness [big size, immensity]
enquire	TRY	ask
ensue	CHANGE TO	follow
ensure [that]	COMPARE	assure [someone that], insure [something]
enter into	CHANGE TO	enter

envisage that	CHANGE TO	think that, expect that
envision	TRY	think, foresee, consider, have in mind
epigram [witty statement]	COMPARE	epigraph [quotation], epitaph [words on tombstone], epithet [characterizing word or phrase]
equable [steady]	COMPARE	equitable [fair]
equally as	CHANGE TO	as, equally, just as
equitable [fair]	COMPARE	equable [steady]
eradicate	TRY	wipe out
ergo [therefore]	CHANGE TO	so, thus, therefore
erstwhile	CHANGE TO	former
eschew	CHANGE TO	avoid
especially	TRY	specially
espouse	CHANGE TO	hold
essential [the adjective]	TRY TO CUT	
essentially	TRY	almost
establish	TRY	set up, find out
et al. [*et alia* = and others]	CHANGE TO	and others
etc. [*et cetera* = and the others]	CHANGE TO	and so on, and so forth
(in the) event that	CHANGE TO	if
eventual	CUT	
eventually	TRY	later
eventuate	CHANGE TO	occur, happen, come about
(it is) evident that	TRY TO CUT	
evince	CHANGE TO	show
evolve	CHANGE TO	change, develop
exacerbate	CHANGE TO	sharpen, make worse
exactly	CUT	
examine	TRY	look at
(for) example	COMPARE	for instance

For consistency, pick one or the other and stick to it,
rather than jumping back and forth between the two.
The preferred usage is
to reserve *example* for *for example*
and *instance* for *in this instance* or *in two instances*.

(for) example	TRY TO CUT	
exceeding	CHANGE TO	more than
(with the) exception of	CHANGE TO	except
(in) excess of	CHANGE TO	over, more than, higher than
exclusively	TRY	only
exhibit [the verb]	TRY	show
(there) exist	CHANGE TO	there are
exist(s)	CHANGE TO	are, is
(the) existence of	CUT	
existing [the adjective]	CUT OR TRY	current
exit [the verb]	CHANGE TO	leave
expedite	CHANGE TO	speed up
expenditure	TRY	cost, expense, spending
expenditures	TRY	expenditure
expense	TRY	cost
expenses	TRY	expense
experience [the verb]	TRY	feel, have, go through
expertise	TRY	talent, know-how, knowledge
explicate	CHANGE TO	explain
expound on	CHANGE TO	expound
extant [still around]	COMPARE	extent [limit, boundary]
extend	TRY	give
extended period	TRY	long period
extent [limit, boundary]	COMPARE	extant [still around]
(the) extent of ~	CHANGE TO	the ~
(to the) extent that	CHANGE TO	as much as, so much that
extinguish	CHANGE TO	put out

F   F   F

facilitate	TRY	ease, help, make easier
facility [a word to avoid]	TRY	plant, warehouse, factory, some other specific word
(as a matter of) fact	CUT	
(the) fact remains that	CUT	
(despite the) fact that	CHANGE TO	although

(due to the) fact that	CHANGE TO	because
(in view of the) fact that	CHANGE TO	because
(the) fact that	CHANGE TO	that
factor [a word to avoid]	TRY	fact, cause, feature, element, consideration
(the ~) factor	CHANGE TO	~

For example:
The efficiency factor is important in manufacturing
should be *Efficiency is important in manufacturing.*

farther [of distance]	COMPARE	further [of time or direction]

The preference is to use *farther* when writing about
physical distances: to go *farther* down the road,
but to go *further* in their studies, to be *further* along in
their studies, and to have a *further* step before
completing their studies. Further, of the two words,
only *further* is used as a verb
and as an adverb in the sense of *moreover.*

fears [the noun]	TRY	fear
feasible [can be done]	COMPARE	possible [can happen]
feasible	TRY	likely, probable, plausible
feel [for emotions]	COMPARE	believe [for convictions], think [for speculations]
fell by 2 percent	CHANGE TO	fell 2 percent
female [the noun]	TRY	woman
fewer (than) [a smaller number of]	COMPARE	less (than) [a smaller amount of]

The preference is to use *fewer* and *fewer than*
with words that have a separate quality
and can be counted, such as persons or fence posts,
and to use *less* and *less than*
with words that have a unitary quality
and cannot be counted, such as water or land.
So: *less land,* but *fewer hectares of land;*
less steel, but *fewer steel mills.* And:
less than a quart, but *fewer than ten quarts.*
There naturally is a middle ground filled

with things that could be considered
either separate or unitary. *Years* is an example.
So take your pick depending on whether you mean the
number of years (*fewer than ten years*)
or the amount of time (*less than ten years*).
And there naturally is an exception:
one less syllable.

(in the) field of	CHANGE TO	in
figurative [metaphorical]	COMPARE	literal [exact]
filled up the ~	CHANGE TO	filled the ~
finalize	CHANGE TO	finish, complete, make final
Finally,...	TRY	Fourth,... or Fifth,...

Finally should be reserved for the last argument,
if it is used at all.

finance [the verb]	TRY	pay for
first began (first started or originated)	CHANGE TO	began (started or originated)
first of all	CHANGE TO	first
firstly	CHANGE TO	first
flaunt [display, show off]	COMPARE	flout [mock, scoff at]
flout [mock, scoff at]	COMPARE	flaunt [display, show off]
focus on	TRY	explore, examine, spotlight, highlight
(as) follow	CHANGE TO	as follows
following [the preposition]	CHANGE TO	after
for example	COMPARE	for instance

See the comments under *example.*

for example	TRY TO CUT	
for the most part	CUT	
for the purpose of	CHANGE TO	for
for the reason that	CHANGE TO	because, since
forceful [having force]	COMPARE	forcible [using force]
forcible [using force]	COMPARE	forceful [having force]
forego [go before]	COMPARE	forgo [relinquish]
foremost	TRY	biggest

(first and) foremost	TRY TO CUT	
(in the) foreseeable future	CHANGE TO	in the future
forgo [relinquish]	COMPARE	forego [go before]
(was in the) form of ~	CHANGE TO	was ~
(a ~ in condensed) form	CHANGE TO	a condensed ~
former [the adjective as noun]	TRY	first

Because the use of *former* and *latter* almost always
forces the reader to go back to see which is which,
it usually is better to repeat the antecedent.
Even if the antecedent is clear,
editors generally prefer to use *first* and *second*.
Never use *former* and *latter*
if there are more than two antecedents:
that is, do not use *former* to refer to the first
of three or more antecedents,
or *latter* to refer to the last of three or more.

forthwith	CHANGE TO	now, immediately
fourthly	CHANGE TO	fourth
frame of reference	TRY TO CUT	
framework	TRY TO CUT	
function [the verb]	TRY	act, live, work, operate
(is a) function of	CHANGE TO	depends on
fund [the verb]	CHANGE TO	pay for
fundamental	CUT OR CHANGE TO	main, basic
fundamentally	CUT	
funding	TRY	money, paying for
funds	CHANGE TO	money
further [of time or direction]	COMPARE	farther [of distance]

See the comments under *farther.*

furthermore	TRY	and

The introductory *furthermore* should be near the end
of the queue of conjunctions that link sentences:
after *and, in addition,* and *moreover.*

(will in the) future	CHANGE TO	will

G	G	G
generally, in general	CUT	
give an indication of	CHANGE TO	indicate
give treatment	CHANGE TO	treat
Given…	TRY	In, Under, Because of
(the figures) given in the table	CHANGE TO	the figures in the table
(a) given piece of	CHANGE TO	a piece of
greater and greater	CHANGE TO	increasing
group of (people)	CHANGE TO	people

H	H	H
(a) half an hour	CHANGE TO	half an hour, a half hour
half of all the ~	CHANGE TO	half the ~
(On the other) hand,…	TRY	But…
have an effect on	CHANGE TO	affect
have an impact on	CHANGE TO	affect
have got to	CHANGE TO	must
(houses) having	TRY	houses that have
(people) having	TRY	people who have
he himself	CHANGE TO	he
healthful [of food or climate]	COMPARE	healthy [of person or animal]
healthy [of person or animal]	COMPARE	healthful [of food or climate]
help make evident	CHANGE TO	make evident
(be) helpful	CHANGE TO	help
hence	TRY	so, thus, therefore
henceforth	CHANGE TO	from now
her	COMPARE	their

To avoid possible sexist references,
the easy solution is to change the pronoun
from singular (*her*) to plural (*their*),
making sure that the antecedent
and the verb number are changed too.

her [of a country]	CHANGE TO	its

her(s) and	CHANGE TO	her, and hers

The problem is with a compound possessive.
Hers and Dr. Boynton's gorilla photographs is wrong.
Her and Dr. Boynton's gorilla photographs
is correct but inelegant.
Her gorilla photographs and Dr. Boynton's
and *Dr. Boynton's gorilla photographs and hers*
are the solutions.

hereby	CUT OR CHANGE TO	now
herein	CUT OR CHANGE TO	here, in this
hereinafter	CHANGE TO	after this
hereof	CUT	
hereto	CUT	
heretofore	CHANGE TO	until now
herewith	CUT OR CHANGE TO	with this
(by) herself	CHANGE TO	alone
(she) herself	CHANGE TO	she
highly unlikely	CHANGE TO	unlikely
(by) himself	CHANGE TO	alone
(he) himself	CHANGE TO	he
his	COMPARE	their

To avoid possible sexist references,
the easy solution is to change the pronoun
from singular (*his*) to plural (*their*),
making sure that the antecedent
and the verb number are changed too.

his and	CHANGE TO	his, and his

See the comments under *her(s) and*.

historic [memorable]	COMPARE	historical [of history]
(an) historic	CHANGE TO	a historic

Before *h*, the preference is to use *a* if the *h* is voiced,
as in *a hotel*, and *an* if it is not,
as in *an hour*.

historically	TRY TO CUT	
hitherto	CHANGE TO	until now, until then

hopefully	CUT	
However, it is going to	CHANGE TO	But it is going to; It is, however, going to
humans	CHANGE TO	human beings, people

I	**I**	**I**

I	COMPARE	we

Do not write *we* if you mean *I*. *In this book we will show* should be *In this book I will show* if there is one author.

ideally	TRY TO CUT OR TRY	preferably
identical to	CHANGE TO	identical with, the same as
idiosyncrasies	CHANGE TO	idiosyncrasy, peculiarities
i.e. [that is]	COMPARE	e.g. [for example]
i.e. [*id est* = that is]	CHANGE TO	that is
if	COMPARE	though

Some writers put an *if* where a *though* is conventional (and preferred): *a cogent statement, if distorted; a cogent statement, though distorted.* Such use of *if* should be avoided because it can change the meaning or give two meanings. *If* should be reserved for introducing a subordinate clause in a conditional sentence:
If writers followed this principle, there would be less confusion.

if	COMPARE	whether

If should be reserved for introducing a subordinate clause in a conditional sentence:
If writers followed this principle, there would be less confusion.
Do not use *if* for *whether: Tell me if you will be going* should be *Tell me whether you will be going.*

If..., then...	CHANGE TO	If...,...
if and when	CHANGE TO	if [possibility], when [temporality]

illusion [visual deception or false perception]	COMPARE	allusion [indirect reference], delusion [deception of belief]
immerse with	CHANGE TO	immerse in
immigrate from	CHANGE TO	immigrate to
impact [the noun]	CHANGE TO	effect

The word *impact* should be reserved for
its literal meaning: *the impact of the stone on the ground.*
If the meaning is figurative—as in *the impact of the
program on the population—effect* is preferred.
The figurative use of *impact* is acceptable when writing
about the effect of effects, writing that usually
deserves rewriting.

impact [the verb]	CHANGE TO	have an effect

Impact is not a verb.

(have an) impact on	CHANGE TO	affect, influence
impede	TRY	stop, hamper, hinder, slow down
(it is) imperative that you	CHANGE TO	you must
implant with	CHANGE TO	implant into
implement	TRY	start, adopt, fulfill, carry out, put into effect
implies	TRY	means
imply [suggest]	COMPARE	infer [conclude]
(is of) importance	CHANGE TO	is critical, is important
(very) important	CHANGE TO	crucial
(More) importantly…	CHANGE TO	More important…
impracticable [of particular acts or things]	COMPARE	impractical [of general actions or things]
impractical [of general actions or things]	COMPARE	impracticable [of particular acts or things]
impressed with	COMPARE	impressed by

A thing is *impressed with* something else;
a person is *impressed by* someone or something,
unless physically *impressed with* something.

(located) in	CHANGE TO	in

in ~ terms	CHANGE TO	~ly
in accordance with	CHANGE TO	by, under, in accord with
in addition	TRY	and, also
in addition to	CHANGE TO	besides
in an effort to	CHANGE TO	to
in cases in which	CHANGE TO	if, when
in connection with	CHANGE TO	on, for, about
in contrast with	CHANGE TO	in contrast to
(~) in depth	TRY TO CUT OR TRY	~ deep
in excess of	CHANGE TO	more than
in fact	CUT	
in instances in which	CHANGE TO	if, when
in keeping with	TRY	in line with
(~) in length	CHANGE TO	~ long
in light of	CHANGE TO	in the light of
in order that ~ might	TRY	for ~ to
in order to ~	CHANGE TO	to ~

The exception is in a sentence that has many *to's*,
giving rise to the need to distinguish the lead
infinitive from other infinitives and from prepositions.
For example: *She had to go to town (in order) to go to the
bank to get some money.* But even in this sentence,
in order can be taken out. If it cannot be taken from a
sentence, the sentence should probably be rewritten.

in particular	CUT	
(the ~) in question	CHANGE TO	the ~, this ~, that ~
in regard to	CHANGE TO	on, about
in relation to	TRY	on, about
in respect to	CHANGE TO	on, about
in spite of	CHANGE TO	despite
in spite of the fact that	CHANGE TO	though, although
in support of	CHANGE TO	to, for
in terms of	TRY	as, at, by, in, of, for, with, under, through

The phrase creeps into too many sentences.
It should be replaced by one of the words on the right
side. If that does not work, try rewriting the sentence.

in that	CUT OR TRY	because
in that case	TRY	then
in that regard	CUT	
in the case of	TRY	by, of, in, for
in the event that	CHANGE TO	if
in the field of	CHANGE TO	in
in the final (last) analysis	CUT	
(was) in the form of ~	CHANGE TO	was ~
(will) in the future	CHANGE TO	will
in the near future	CHANGE TO	soon
in the neighborhood of	TRY	about
in the past was	CHANGE TO	was
in the region of	CHANGE TO	near, about, close to
in the sense that	TRY	in that
in the vicinity of	CHANGE TO	near, about, close to
in the way of	TRY	in
in this case	TRY TO CUT	
in this connection	CHANGE TO	about
in toto [on the whole]	CHANGE TO	totally, completely, entirely
in turn	CUT	
in view of	TRY	because
in view of the fact that	CHANGE TO	because
(~) in width	CHANGE TO	~ wide
in~	COMPARE	un~, non~, not

Tacking *non* on the front of a word is the easiest and sloppiest way to make an antonym.
First, try a true antonym: *obscure* to *clear.*
Second, try an antonym created by the prefixes *in* and *un*: *unclear* to *clear, insubstantial* to *substantial.*
Third, try *not*: *not transparent* to *transparent, not alone* to *alone.* Fourth, having exhausted these possibilities, use *non.* If you must use the prefix *non*, do not insert a hyphen: *non-essential* should be *nonessential.*
The exception is when *non* precedes a capitalized word or a hyphenated construction: *non-English-speaking people.*

inasmuch as	CHANGE TO	because
incidence of	TRY TO CUT	

include [some parts]	COMPARE	comprise [all parts]
included in	CHANGE TO	in
including	TRY	and, among them
incorporated	TRY	of, used, part of
increase [the noun or intransitive verb]	TRY	rise
incredible [hard to believe]	COMPARE	incredulous [skeptical]

Things, events, and actions can be *incredible* to people;
only people can be *incredulous* about something.

incredulous [skeptical]	COMPARE	incredible [hard to believe]

See the comments under *incredible*.

inculcate with	CHANGE TO	inculcate in or into
indebtedness	CHANGE TO	debt
indeed	TRY TO CUT	
independent from	CHANGE TO	independent of
independently	CHANGE TO	on its own, on their own
independently of	CHANGE TO	independent of
indicate	TRY	say, show, mean, suggest
indication	TRY	sign, gauge
(is) indicative of	TRY	indicates
indicia	CHANGE TO	signs
individual	TRY	person
individual projects	CHANGE TO	projects
inevitably	CUT	
infer [conclude]	COMPARE	imply [suggest]
infinitely more	CHANGE TO	much more
inflict with	CHANGE TO	inflict on
inform	CHANGE TO	tell, write
infringe on (upon)	CHANGE TO	infringe [violate]
ingenious [clever]	COMPARE	ingenuous [naive, natural]
ingenuous [naive, natural]	COMPARE	ingenious [clever]
inherent in	CHANGE TO	in
inherently	CUT	
initial	TRY	first

initially	TRY	at first
initiate	CHANGE TO	start or begin
inject with	CHANGE TO	inject into
inquire	CHANGE TO	ask
inside of [the preposition]	CHANGE TO	inside
insight	TRY	understanding
insight into	TRY	idea about
insofar as [because]	TRY	because
insofar as [to the extent that]	TRY	so far as
Insofar as ~ is concerned,	CHANGE TO	In, Of, On, For, or About ~ ,
insoluble [of substances or problems]	COMPARE	unsolvable [of problems]
(for) instance	COMPARE	for example

See the comments under *example.*

(in most) instances	TRY	most ~s
(in) instances in which	CHANGE TO	if, when
instead of ~	CHANGE TO	rather than ~
instill with	CHANGE TO	instill into
institute [the verb]	CHANGE TO	start or set up
(was) instrumental in ~ing	CHANGE TO	helped ~
(will be) instrumental in ~ing	CHANGE TO	will help ~
insufficient	TRY	not enough
insure [something]	COMPARE	assure [someone that], ensure [that]
integral part	TRY	part
integrate	TRY	mix, join, combine, amalgamate
integrate into	CHANGE TO	integrate with
intense	COMPARE	intensive

Close in meaning, the two words are often misused as
synonyms. The distinction that sometimes helps is to
reserve *intense* for passive things,
intensive for active things:
something is *intense*, something applied is *intensive.*
Thus: *War is intense*, but *bombing is intensive.*

The considerable overlap in usage blurs the
distinction, however.

intensive	COMPARE	intense
inter alia [among other things]	CHANGE TO	among others
(of) interest	TRY	relevant
interestingly	CUT	
interface	CHANGE TO	cooperate, work together (unless writing about systems)
into	TRY	in
investigation into	CHANGE TO	investigation of
investments	TRY	investment
involve [a word to avoid]	TRY TO CUT	

The word should seldom replace
or be combined with a preposition.
The government agencies involved in carrying out
should be *The government agencies carrying out.*
The policies involving several departments
should be *The policies of several departments.*
If a verb or participle must stand, try to find a more
precise word, such as *mean, affect,* or *include.*

(the costs) involved in ~	TRY	the cost of ~
irregardless	CHANGE TO	regardless
is	COMPARE	are

See the comments under *are.*

is because	CHANGE TO	is that, is caused by
(in) isolation	CUT OR CHANGE TO	alone
it	TRY TO CUT	

The presence of *it* in a sentence
is a signal to look for problems:
having two *it*'s referring to more than one antecedent;
having no obvious antecedent; having a wordy
construction that serves little purpose,
such as those that follow.

It appears that…	CUT	

It can be stated with certainty that...	CUT	
It goes without saying that...	CUT	
It is apparent that...	CUT	
It is important to note that...	CUT	
It is to be hoped that...	CHANGE TO	I hope...
It is worth noting that...	CUT	
It is ~ that is...	CHANGE TO	~ is...
It is ~ which is...	CHANGE TO	~ is...
It should be noted that...	CUT	
It should be pointed out that...	CUT	
It will be noted that...	CUT	
It would appear that...	CUT	
its	COMPARE	it's

People still confuse the contraction *it's* (it is) and
the possessive *its* (*its'* is not a word).

(by) itself	CHANGE TO	alone
(the ~) itself	CHANGE TO	the ~
-ize [avoid, as in *prioritize*]	TRY TO CUT	

J   J   J

join together	CHANGE TO	join
judicial [of courts]	COMPARE	judicious [of wisdom]
judicious [of wisdom]	COMPARE	judicial [of courts]
(at this or that) juncture	CHANGE TO	now, then

K   K   K

key [the adjective, a word to avoid]	TRY TO CUT OR TRY	main, important

The word *key* is defensible if it is for opening
a real or metaphorical lock.

(is the) key	TRY	is important
(these or those) kinds of ~s	CHANGE TO	this kind of ~, these kinds of ~, that kind of ~, those kinds of ~

The plural is often unnecessary: *these kinds of problems*
should usually be *this kind of problem*
or *these kinds of problem; those kinds of problems*
should usually be *that kind of problem*
or *those kinds of problem.*
Some editors prefer to rescue the noun
from the prepositional phrase by writing
problems of this (or that) kind.

known as	CUT

L   L   L

lack of	TRY	without
(a) large part of	CHANGE TO	many, much
(a) large percentage of	CHANGE TO	many, much
(a) large proportion of	CHANGE TO	many, much
large-sized ~	TRY	large ~
largely	CUT	
last but not least	CUT OR CHANGE TO	finally
lastly	CUT OR CHANGE TO	finally, last
later on	TRY	later
latter [the adjective as noun]	TRY	last, second

See the comments under *former.*

latter half	TRY	second half
latter part	TRY	later part
laudable [worthy of praise]	COMPARE	laudatory [expressing praise]
laudatory [expressing praise]	COMPARE	laudable [worthy of praise]
lay [put to rest]	COMPARE	lie [be at or come to rest]

Problems arise with the past tense and past participle.
For *lay,* the past tense and participle is *laid.*

Thus: *I think I laid the flowers on the table yesterday,*
but I could have laid them there the day before.
For *lie,* the past tense is *lay,* the past participle *lain.*
Thus: *The flowers lay on the table until I picked them up;*
they could have lain there forever.

lay out [the verb]	TRY	lay
led to increased competition	CHANGE TO	increased the competition
(~ in) length	CHANGE TO	~ long
lengthy	CHANGE TO	long
less (than) [a smaller amount of]	COMPARE	fewer (than) [a smaller number of]

See the comments under *fewer.*

let us	CUT	
(the) level of ~	TRY	the ~

Unless writing about a liquid or hierarchy,
try to cut *level:*
the spending is better than *the level of spending;*
the local people is better than *the people at the local level.*

liable	TRY	likely
licence	CHANGE TO	license
lie [be at or come to rest]	COMPARE	lay [put to rest]

See the comments under *lay.*

(in) lieu of	CHANGE TO	rather than
like	COMPARE	as, as if, such as

See the comments under *as.*

(and the) like	CUT	
likely	TRY	probable (probably)
likewise	CHANGE TO	so, also
limitation	TRY	limit
limited	TRY	few, small, meager
linkage	TRY	link
literal [exact]	COMPARE	figurative [metaphorical]
literally	TRY TO CUT	
little	TRY	few, limited

loan [the verb]	CHANGE TO	lend
locality [location]	TRY	place
locate	TRY	find
located at (or in)	CHANGE TO	at, in
lose out on	CHANGE TO	lose
(a) lot of	TRY	much, many
loth	CHANGE TO	loath
lots of	TRY	much, many
luxuriant [abundant]	COMPARE	luxurious [of luxury]
luxurious [of luxury]	COMPARE	luxuriant [abundant]

M   M   M

(decisions) made by	CHANGE TO	decisions by
made up out of	CHANGE TO	made of
magnitude	TRY	size, extent
(the) magnitude of ~	CHANGE TO	the ~
mainly	CUT	
major [great, greater]	TRY	big, main, chief, great, important, principal
(the) majority of	CHANGE TO	many, most, most of
make a decision about	CHANGE TO	decide about
make an appearance	CHANGE TO	appear
make changes	CHANGE TO	change
male [the noun]	TRY	man
manage to (do so)	CHANGE TO	do so
manner	TRY	way
many of the ~	TRY	many ~
marginal	COMPARE	small

Do not use *marginal* if you mean *small.*
Marginal refers to increments at the margin or
to something at a dividing line.

marginally	CHANGE TO	slightly
masterful [strong-willed]	COMPARE	masterly [skillful]
masterly [skillful]	COMPARE	masterful [strong-willed]
match up	CHANGE TO	match
maximal	TRY	big, full, high, large, most

maximize [make most]	TRY	raise, increase
(is) maximized	CHANGE TO	is most, is greatest
maximum [the most]	TRY	much, most, greatest
may [permission]	COMPARE	can [ability], might [possibility]
may possibly	CHANGE TO	may, might, could
meaningful	CUT	
means	TRY	way
(by) means of	TRY	by
means to produce	CHANGE TO	means of producing, way to produce
media is	CHANGE TO	media are
medium [the adjective]	COMPARE	medium-size

One tendency is to equate *medium* with *small* and *large:*
small and medium firms should be
small and medium-size firms;
medium-size and large-size firms should be
large and medium-size firms.

methodology [study of method]	COMPARE	method [way to do something]
might [possibility]	COMPARE	can [ability], may [permission]
might possibly	CHANGE TO	might, could
minimal [the least possible]	TRY	low, small, little, least
minimize [make least]	TRY	lower, reduce, decrease
(is) minimized	CHANGE TO	is least, lowest, smallest
minimum [least]	TRY	least, little, lowest, smallest
minor [small]	TRY	small, unimportant
(the) minority of	TRY	few, some
miss out on	CHANGE TO	miss
mitigate against	CHANGE TO	militate against [make unlikely] or mitigate [reduce]
mode	CHANGE TO	way, method
modicum	CHANGE TO	some
modus	CHANGE	way of
moment in time	TRY	time

moneys	CHANGE TO	money
more and more	TRY	more
more or less	TRY TO CUT	
more substantial	CHANGE TO	greater
more than [for an amount]	COMPARE	over [for a position]

Write *over the table* or *over the moon,*
but *more than a dollar, more than 20 percent,*
and *more than five hundred years.*

mostly	CUT	
motivate	TRY	make, cause
motivation	TRY	drive, reason
multitude of ~s	TRY	many (or several) ~s
must inevitably	CHANGE TO	must
must necessarily	CHANGE TO	must
mutual [reciprocated]	COMPARE	common [of many]
my (mine) and	CHANGE TO	my, and mine

See the comments under *her(s) and.*

N   N   N

namely	CUT	
naturally	CUT	
nature [a word to avoid]	TRY TO CUT	

As with *case* and *character,* the word is best avoided.
Here are the most common abuses
and the ways around them:
the secret nature of should be *the secrecy of;*
the nature of the work is secret
and *the work is of a secret nature*
should be *the work is secret.*

(is of a ~) nature	CHANGE TO	is ~
(in the) near future	TRY	soon
necessarily	TRY TO CUT	
necessary	TRY	needed

necessitate	TRY	need, require
necessity	TRY	need, requirement
needless to say	CUT	
(in the) negative	CHANGE TO	no
(in the) neighborhood of [about]	CHANGE TO	about
neither a, b, nor c	CHANGE TO	Of a, b, and c, none...

Many editors dislike the use of *neither-nor* with
more than two elements.
There naturally are some outstanding
exceptions: *Neither rain, sleet, snow, and so on.*

neither of them are	CHANGE TO	neither of them is
never the less	CHANGE TO	nevertheless
nevertheless	COMPARE	nonetheless

Take your pick and stick to it.

nevertheless	TRY	but, even so
no doubt	TRY TO CUT	
non~	TRY	in~, un~, not

See the comments under *in~*.

none	COMPARE	not one

The decision to use one or the other
turns on whether emphasis is wanted:
not one is more emphatic than *none.*

none of them are	CHANGE TO	none of them is
none the less	CHANGE TO	nonetheless
nor	COMPARE	or

Nor is acceptable as the correlative conjunction
with *neither* or at the beginning of a negative sentence
that follows a negative sentence:
They did not go to the beach.
Nor did they go to the mountains.
Many people incorrectly use *nor*
as a conjunction after a negative verb:
They did not go to the beach nor the mountains.
Or should replace *nor* in the example.

not a	TRY	no
not necessarily	CHANGE TO	not always
not...nor	CHANGE TO	not...or
not only..., but also	TRY TO CUT OR TRY	not only..., but...

Much overused as correlative conjunctions,
not only and *but also* should be used sparingly
and only with compound sentences.
The concert was not only long, but also boring
should be either *The concert was long and boring*
or *Not only was the concert long; it was boring.*
These correlatives are also a favorite in sentences
that begin with *It: It is not only unsurprising,*
but also expected, that could just as easily be
It is unsurprising, even expected, that,
which could even be *It is expected that.*

| not the same | CHANGE TO | different |
| not un~ | CHANGE TO | ~ |

Recall Orwell's complaint:
A not unblack dog was chasing a not unsmall rabbit
across a not ungreen field.

notwithstanding	TRY	despite
nowadays	TRY	today
number [a word to avoid]	TRY TO CUT	
(a) number of	CUT OR CHANGE TO	some, many, several, forty-three

Improve such constructions as *a number of firms*
by writing *some firms, many firms,*
several firms, or *forty-three firms.*
If it is not possible to be more precise,
simply write *firms.*
Change such constructions as
ten times the number of jobs
to *ten times the jobs.*

(a large) number of	CHANGE TO	many
(a small) number of	CHANGE TO	some
numerous	CHANGE TO	many

O	O	O
objective [the noun]	TRY	end, aim, purpose
oblivious to	TRY	oblivious of
obtain	TRY	get
obverse	COMPARE	converse, reverse

See the comments under *converse.*

obverse [front of coin]	COMPARE	reverse [back of coin]
obviously	CUT	
occur	TRY TO CUT	

As with *make,* constructions with *occur* often are
larded: *The committee's actions occurred on*
should be *The committee acted on.*

of course	CUT	
(is) of importance	CHANGE TO	is important
off of	CHANGE TO	off, from
offers comparisons	CHANGE TO	compares
oftentimes	CHANGE TO	often
on a regular basis	CHANGE TO	regularly
on an annual basis	CHANGE TO	yearly, annually, once a year
on the basis of	TRY	by, on, because of
on the one hand	CUT	
on the order of	CHANGE TO	about
On the other hand...	CHANGE TO	Yet..., But...
on the part of	TRY	by, of, from
once and for all	TRY	definitively
one [the impersonal pronoun]	CUT	

One does need to get exercise in the tropics, doesn't one?
For if one doesn't, it is very easy for one to go crackers.
It usually is better to use another pronoun,
such as *you,* or to write generally, using *people.*

(the list is a long) one	CHANGE TO	the list is long
(the list is not a complete) one	CHANGE TO	the list is not complete

one half, one third, and so on	COMPARE	one-half, one-third, and so on

Pick one style of writing fractions and stick to it, except for the variations on the right side of the next entry.

one-half, one-third, and so on	TRY	a half, a third, and so on
opening up to	CHANGE TO	opening to
opt for	CHANGE TO	choose
optimal	TRY	best, most, better, greatest
optimize	TRY	make best, most, and so on
optimum	TRY	best
or [as in and/or]	CUT	
oral [of mouth]	COMPARE	verbal [of words]
(on the) order of	CHANGE TO	about
order of magnitude	CUT	
(in) order that ~ might	TRY	for ~ to
(in) order to ~	CHANGE TO	to ~

See the comments under *in order to.*

organizational structure	TRY	organization
orientate	CHANGE TO	orient
originate from	CHANGE TO	come from
(On the) other hand,...	CHANGE TO	But,...
other than	TRY	except
our(s)	CHANGE TO	our, and ours

See the comments under *her(s) and.*

out of four	CHANGE TO	of four
(starting) out with	CHANGE TO	starting with
outside of	CHANGE TO	outside
over [for a position]	COMPARE	more than [for an amount]

See the comments under *more than.*

(when the ~ was) over	CHANGE TO	after the ~
over time	CUT	

Overall,	TRY TO CUT	
overall	COMPARE	whole, total, entire, average, aggregate
(the) overall ~	TRY	the ~
overly	CHANGE TO	too, too much
owing to	TRY	caused by, because of
owing to the fact that	CHANGE TO	because
own [the adjective]	TRY TO CUT	

His own car should be *his car.*

P	P	P
parameter	TRY	limit, boundary, condition
(a large) part of	CHANGE TO	much, many
(a small) part of	CHANGE TO	some
(on the) part of	TRY	by, of, from
partake in	CHANGE TO	partake of
partially	TRY	partly
(this or that) particular ~	CHANGE TO	this (or that) ~
particularly	CUT	
party	TRY	person
(in the) past was	TRY	was
(to) pay off	CHANGE TO	to pay, to repay
pending	TRY	until
people [in general]	COMPARE	persons [in particular]
peoples	CHANGE TO	people
per	TRY	a

Barrels per day or *barrels a day; dollars per year* or
dollars a year; GNP per person or *GNP a person;*
rate per hour or *rate an hour.*
Many writers use *per* all the time;
some editors push for using *a (an)* all the time.
The best practice probably is to use *a* much of the time
and to resort to *per* if *a* sounds unnatural.

(as) per	CHANGE TO	on, for, about, further to, in accord with
per annum	CHANGE TO	a year

per capita	CHANGE TO	a person
per se	CUT	
percent	COMPARE	percentage point

If the change is in a rate, it is a *percentage point* change.
For example, *The GNP growth rate increased
2 percentage points.*

(25) percent	CHANGE TO	a quarter
(50) percent	CHANGE TO	half
(100) percent	CHANGE TO	all
(a) percent of ~	CHANGE TO	a percentage of ~, a proportion of ~
(a) percentage of	CHANGE TO	part of
(a large) percentage of	CHANGE TO	much, many
(a small) percentage of	CHANGE TO	some
(over a) period of three years	CHANGE TO	over three years
period of time	CHANGE TO	time, period
persons [in particular]	COMPARE	people [in general]
persuade [someone of, to, or that]	COMPARE	convince [someone of or that]

There is much overlap except before *to*,
where only *persuade* will do.
See the comments under *convince.*

pertaining to	CHANGE TO	about
pertains to	CHANGE TO	is about
peruse	CHANGE TO	read
(this) phenomena	CHANGE TO	this phenomenon
plays a major role	TRY	contributes to, is important
plus	TRY	and
(at this) point in time	CHANGE TO	now, at this point, at this time
(the) point is that	CUT	
point of view	TRY	view, viewpoint
(from the) point of view of ~	CHANGE TO	for ~
policy	TRY TO CUT	
population	TRY	people
portion	CHANGE TO	part

posterior to	CHANGE TO	after
potential [the noun]	TRY TO CUT	
potential gains	TRY	possible gains
practicable [of particular acts or things]	COMPARE	practical [of general actions or things]
practical [of general actions or things	COMPARE	practicable [of particular acts or things]
practically	CHANGE TO	almost, nearly
pre~ [as in preprocessing]	CHANGE TO	before processing
preceding [the one just passed]	COMPARE	previous [past]
precipitate [rash, abrupt]	COMPARE	precipitous [steep]
precipitous [steep]	COMPARE	precipitate [rash, abrupt]
precise(ly)	CUT	
predicated on	CHANGE TO	based on
prefer ~ over	CHANGE TO	prefer ~ to
preferable	CHANGE TO	best, better, preferred
preliminary to	CHANGE TO	before
preparatory to	CHANGE TO	before
(is) prepared to	CHANGE TO	is ready (or willing) to
(is a) prerequisite for	TRY	is needed for
prescribe [dictate or ordain]	COMPARE	proscribe [outlaw or prohibit]
(at) present	CUT OR CHANGE TO	now, today
(the) present ~	CHANGE TO	this ~

The seeming need for *present* comes from
the requirement to distinguish, say, two other books
from this one, unnecessarily called *the present book.*

(the) present writer	CHANGE TO	I
presented in this ~	CHANGE TO	in this ~
presently	CHANGE TO	now, soon
pressures	TRY	pressure
presumably	TRY	probably
pretty [the weak intensifier]	CUT	
prevalent	TRY	common
preventative	CHANGE TO	preventive
previous [past]	COMPARE	preceding [the one just passed]

previous to	CHANGE TO	before
previously	CHANGE TO	before, earlier
(have) previously received	CHANGE TO	have received
primarily	TRY	mainly
principal(ly)	TRY	main(ly) or chief(ly)
prior [the adjective]	TRY	earlier
prior experience	CHANGE TO	experience
prior to	CHANGE TO	before
prioritize [and similar barbarisms]	CHANGE TO	set priorities for
priority [a word to avoid]	TRY TO CUT	
proceed	CHANGE TO	go, continue, go ahead
process [a word to avoid]	TRY TO CUT	
(the) process of, say, modernization	CHANGE TO	modernization
(the decision-making) process	CHANGE TO	decision-making
procure	CHANGE TO	get
pronounced [the adjective]	CHANGE TO	great
proper	TRY TO CUT	
prophecy [the noun]	COMPARE	prophesy [the verb]
prophesy [the verb]	COMPARE	prophecy [the noun]
proportion	CHANGE TO	part
(the greater) proportion of	CHANGE TO	most
(a large) proportion of	CHANGE TO	much, many
(a small) proportion of	CHANGE TO	some
proscribe [outlaw or prohibit]	COMPARE	prescribe [dictate or ordain]
proven	TRY	proved

The past tense and past participle of *prove* is *proved*,
not *proven*, but *proven* has invaded the place of *proved*
in speech, and thus in much writing:
until proven guilty; proven oil reserves.
Proved is the correct word in both examples.

proves to be	CHANGE TO	is
provide	TRY	give, have, offer

provide a summary	COMPARE	summarize

A person *provides a summary* by handing or sending one to another person. A person (or introduction or conclusion) *summarizes* by drawing the main points together for an audience or reader.

provided (providing) that	TRY	if

The change should always be made
in introductory clauses of stipulation:
Provided (that) she goes should be *If she goes.*

(in close) proximity to	CHANGE TO	near, close to
purchase [the verb]	CHANGE TO	buy
purely	CUT	
(for the) purpose of	CHANGE TO	for, to

For the purpose of getting to work on time
should be *To get to work on time.*

(with the) purpose of ~ing	CHANGE TO	to ~
pursue	TRY	follow
put differently	TRY	in other words

Q   Q   Q

qua	CHANGE TO	as
quasi-money	CHANGE TO	quasi money
quasi public body	CHANGE TO	quasi-public body
(the ~ in) question	CHANGE TO	the ~, this ~, that ~,
(the) question of whether	CHANGE TO	whether, the question whether
quite	CUT	
quite a few	CHANGE TO	many
quote [the noun]	CHANGE TO	quotation

Quote is a verb, not a noun:
The quote is from a column by William Raspberry should be
The quotation is from a column by William Raspberry.

R	R	R
ranging from…to	TRY	including
rapidity	CHANGE TO	speed
(but) rather	CHANGE TO	but
Rather,…	CHANGE TO	Instead,…
rather [the modifier]	CUT	
rationale	TRY	plan, reason, thinking
rationalize	TRY	explain away
re	CUT OR CHANGE TO	about
reach a conclusion	CHANGE TO	conclude
(the conclusion) reached	CHANGE TO	the conclusion
reaction	TRY	response, impression
real	TRY TO CUT	
(the) reason is because	CHANGE TO	the reason is that
(by) reason of	CHANGE TO	because of
(for the) reason that	CHANGE TO	because, since
(the) reason why	TRY	the reason, the reason that, the reason for ~ to be
receive	TRY	get, have
(is the) recipient of	CHANGE TO	got
redolent with	CHANGE TO	redolent of
reduce (reduction)	TRY	cut
refer [directly]	COMPARE	allude [refer indirectly]
refer back	CHANGE TO	refer
(with) reference to	CHANGE TO	of, on, for, about
reflect	TRY	show
(in) regard to	CHANGE TO	on, about
(with) regard to	CHANGE TO	of, on, for, about
regarding	TRY	on, for, about
(as) regards	CHANGE TO	in, on, for, about
(in the) region of	CHANGE TO	near, about, close to
relate	TRY	say, tell
related to	TRY	of, has to do with
relates to	TRY	of, on, about
relating to	TRY	on, for, about
relation	COMPARE	relationship

Some people use these words as synonyms.
One way to differentiate them is to use them thus:
The *relationship* between the United States and Western
Europe; East-West *relations;*
the *relationship* between two people;
a person's *relatives*, not *relations;* the *relation* between
exports and gross national product; and so on.
There is nothing hard and fast to disentangle usage,
except to prefer the shorter word.

(in) relation to	TRY	on, about
relationship	COMPARE	relation

See the comments under *relation.*

relative(ly)	TRY TO CUT	
rely upon	CHANGE TO	rely on
remuneration (remunerations)	CHANGE TO	pay
render	CHANGE TO	give, make
replace	COMPARE	substitute

The prepositions determine the use of these
seeming synonyms: *replace X by Y*, not *replace X for Y;*
substitute X for Y, not *substitute X by Y.*

replicate	TRY	copy, reproduce
reportedly	CUT	
represents	TRY	is, makes up
require	TRY	need, want, call for
requirement	TRY	need
requisite [the adjective]	CHANGE TO	needed
requisite [the noun]	CHANGE TO	needed thing
reside	TRY	live
(in or with) respect to	CHANGE TO	on, for, about
respective(ly)	TRY TO CUT	

If the links between the elements of a sentence are
ambiguous, rewrite it.
The most common rewrite is from
*Bob turned fifty and Alice turned forty in 1992
and in 1993, respectively* to
Bob turned fifty in 1992, and Alice turned forty in 1993.

result in [the verb]   CHANGE TO   lead to

The reasons are that *lead to* saves a syllable
and avoids possible confusion with the noun *result*.

(as a) result of	CHANGE TO	from, because of
reveal	TRY	show
revenues	CHANGE TO	revenue
reverse	COMPARE	converse, obverse

See the comments under *converse*.

| reverse [back of coin] | COMPARE | obverse [front of coin] |
| role | TRY TO CUT OR TRY | importance |

Many editors feel that *roles* should be reserved
for the stage. The standard change is from
The role of the vaccine in eradicating polio
to *The importance of the vaccine in eradicating polio.*
But it is not always that easy.

| role to play in | TRY TO CUT | |
| rose by 2 percent | CHANGE TO | rose 2 percent |

This change does not work for fractions.
In *rose by half* the *by* must stand.

S	S	S
~s'	CHANGE TO	~s's
~'s	COMPARE	of ~

The possessive form is fine for people,
but if extended, say, to countries, it introduces what
Follett calls the false possessive. *Brazil's GNP* is an illogical construction because Brazil is incapable of possessing a GNP. The phrase should be rewritten as *the GNP of Brazil.* Or so the logic goes. The logic nevertheless breaks down with *its*, which is fine as an inanimate possessive: *its population.* The best practice is to avoid false possessives in scholarly writing and to avoid excessive use of false possessives in other writing.

safely (assume)	CHANGE TO	assume
said	COMPARE	wrote, written
(not the) same	CHANGE TO	different
savings	COMPARE	saving

The general preference is to use *savings* as an adjective,
saving as a noun: *savings accounts* and *savings rates*,
but *national saving* and *the rate of saving*.
There naturally is a middle ground of confusion,
such as with *a family's savings* and *a saving grace*.
But the general preference is worth keeping in mind.
So is the idea of trying to make plural nouns singular.

..., say, of five years	CHANGE TO	...of, say, five years
secondly	CHANGE TO	second
sector	TRY TO CUT	
secure [the verb]	CHANGE TO	get
seek	CHANGE TO	try, look for
seem(s)	COMPARE	is, are
semiannually	TRY	twice a year
semi-detached	CHANGE TO	semidetached

The general preference is to run the prefix *semi* solid.
Some editors run it solid only before consonants,
hyphenating it before a vowel, as in *semi-industrial*.

semimonthly	TRY	twice a month
semiweekly	TRY	twice a week
(a) series of	TRY TO CUT	
serve to ~	CHANGE TO	~s
set forth	CHANGE TO	give
shall	CHANGE TO	will

Shall can be forgotten in today's writing.
But if you want to preserve the distinction between
shall and *will*, see Strunk and White.

she [of a country]	CHANGE TO	it
she herself	CHANGE TO	she
should	TRY	would
significant [of statistical relations and things signified]	COMPARE	big, large, important

| (a) significant degree of | CUT | |
| since | COMPARE | because |

> Some editors, in the interest of not putting readers
> on the wrong scent, reserve *because* for cause and *since*
> for time: *Because I am going*, but *Since 1941*. The wrong
> scent is evident in such a construction as *Since I have
> been going*, which could relate to cause or to time.

(a) single ~	TRY	one ~
situated in	CHANGE TO	in
skills	TRY	skill
(a) small part of	CHANGE TO	some
(a) small percentage of	CHANGE TO	some
(a) small proportion of	CHANGE TO	some
small-sized	CHANGE TO	small
So	TRY TO CUT	

> Useful but often overused as a conjunction.

| so as not to ~ | CHANGE TO | to ~ |

> The words that fill in the blanks must be opposites,
> which an example can make clear:
> *so as not to obscure* is longer than but equal to *to clarify*.

| so as to | CHANGE TO | to |
| so long as | COMPARE | as long as |

> See the comments under *as long as*.

so-called	CUT	
socioeconomic	TRY	social and economic
soluble [of substances or problems]	COMPARE	solvable [of problems]
solvable [of problems]	COMPARE	soluble [of substances or problems]
some	TRY TO CUT	
some of the ~	CHANGE TO	some ~s
somewhat	CUT	
sought	CHANGE TO	tried, looked for
specific	TRY TO CUT	

> *A specific program* is usually the same as *a program*.

(in) spite of	CHANGE TO	despite
(in) spite of the fact that	CHANGE TO	(al)though
stanch [the verb]	COMPARE	staunch [the adjective]
(by any) standard	CUT	
(from the) standpoint of	CHANGE TO	for
start up	TRY	start
starting out with	CHANGE TO	starting with
state [the verb]	CHANGE TO	say
staunch [the adjective]	COMPARE	stanch [the verb]
(will take) steps to ~	CHANGE TO	will ~
still remain	CHANGE TO	remain
straightforward	TRY	clear
strategic	TRY TO CUT	
strategy	TRY	plan, technique
strictly speaking	CUT	
(to) subject to tax	CHANGE TO	to tax
(is) subjected to tax	CHANGE TO	is taxed

The formula is to cut *subject(ed) to*
and to change the noun to a verb.
It does not always work.

subsequent	CHANGE TO	later
subsequent to	CHANGE TO	after
subsequently	CHANGE TO	later, then
substitute	COMPARE	replace

See the comments under *replace*.

succeed in ~ing	CHANGE TO	~
successfully	CUT	
such as	COMPARE	like

See the comments under *as*.

(~s,) such as...	TRY	such ~s as...

This change can do away with two commas
and improve cadence, but it cannot always be made.
*Leading oil companies, such as Exxon, Mobil, and British
Petroleum, are...* could be written *Such leading oil
companies as Exxon, Mobil, and British Petroleum are....*

The change seems to work best if the noun
exemplified is general and not specific,
worst if the noun is particular, preceded by *the.*

such as X, Y, Z, and so on	CHANGE TO	such as X, Y, and Z
(on) such factors as ~	TRY	on, say, ~
(until) such time as	CHANGE TO	until
sufficient(ly)	TRY	enough
suggest	TRY	say
(the) sum of $1 million	CHANGE TO	$1 million
sum total	CHANGE TO	total
(in) support of	CHANGE TO	to, for
supposing (supposing that)	CHANGE TO	if
systematically	CUT	

T   **T**   **T**

take account of	COMPARE	take into account

Use one or the other.

take action	CHANGE TO	act
take into account	COMPARE	take account of

Use one or the other.

(will) take steps to	CHANGE TO	will
(both facts) taken together	CHANGE TO	both facts
(is) tantamount to	CHANGE TO	means
target [a word to avoid]	TRY	aim, goal, objective
tells us	TRY	suggests
tend to	TRY TO CUT	
(have a) tendency to	CHANGE TO	tend to
terminate	TRY	end
termination	TRY	ending
terminology	TRY	terms
(in) ~ terms	TRY	~ly
(in) terms of	TRY	by, in, of, for, with, under, through, in relation to

The construction should seldom be permitted to stand.
In terms of value added should be *In value added.*
Explain in terms of should be *Explain by.* Another way
around *in terms of* is rewriting the sentence.

thankfully	CUT	
that	COMPARE	which

The important things are knowing why you use one or
the other and punctuating *which* clauses correctly.
See chapter 7.

that is (are)	TRY TO CUT

Try to delete *that is (are)* in a restrictive clause:
An item that is exported is the same as
but longer than *An item exported.*
The same goes for *Factors that are deleterious to,*
which can be cut to *Factors deleterious to.*

the [particular]	COMPARE	a, an [general]

See the comments under *a, an.*

the ~ of	TRY	~ing

The phrase *the manufacture of* can almost always be
changed to *manufacturing, the production of* to *producing.*
The same goes in spades for
the manufacturing of and *the producing of.*

the fact that	TRY	that
their(s) and	CHANGE TO	their, and theirs

See the comments under *her(s) and.*

(by) themselves	TRY	alone
(the ~s) themselves	CHANGE TO	the ~s
There are four reasons for...	CHANGE TO	The four reasons for...

This is one of the most common changes by editors.
The formula, with a *There are* opening followed by
an adjective and noun, is to pull the noun ahead
of the verb to replace *There.*

there are now	CHANGE TO	there are

The tense of the verb usually is enough to indicate
time and to make the adverb redundant.
The same thing happens with
there were in the past and *there will be in the future.*
But not with *yesterday, today,* and *tomorrow*
if they refer to days.

there exist	CHANGE TO	there are
thereafter	CHANGE TO	then, after that
thereby	CHANGE TO	by it, by that

Better still, change the construction
from passive to active:
from *the changes indicated thereby*
to *the changes indicated by it* to *the changes it indicates.*
Two birds, one stone.

therefor	CHANGE TO	for it
therefore	TRY	so, thus
therefrom	CHANGE TO	from it
therein	CHANGE TO	there, in it
thereof	CHANGE TO	its, of it
thereto	CHANGE TO	to it, about it
thereupon	CHANGE TO	then
therewith	CHANGE TO	with it
these kinds of ~s	CHANGE TO	this kind of ~, these kinds of ~

The plural is often unnecessary: *these kinds of problems*
should usually be *this kind of problem* or *these kinds of
problem.* Some editors prefer to rescue the noun from
the prepositional phrase by writing *problems of this kind.*

(for one) thing	CUT	
think [for speculations]	COMPARE	feel [for emotions], believe [for convictions]
thirdly	CHANGE TO	third
This...	COMPARE	The...

It often happens in consecutive sentences that the
subject of one is, say, *This distinction* or *That* referring

to the distinction. What is to be done if the subject of
the next sentence is the same?
This distinction would be repetitive, which is not bad.
That would be ambiguous, which is bad.
Clear and elegant, however, is *The distinction*, more so
than *Such a distinction*, which is another possibility.

this means that	TRY	so
this (that) particular ~	CHANGE TO	this (that) ~
this type of	TRY	such
thorough	CUT	
those ~ in which	CHANGE TO	~ which
those ~ that	CHANGE TO	~ that, those that

Those restricts the noun it precedes,
just as a *that* clause restricts the noun it follows.
To use both is to be doubly restrictive, which is not
necessary. The solution is to cut *those* or to cut the
noun and have the adjective as a substantive pronoun:
those bundles of kindling that we sold
should be *(the) bundles of kindling that we sold*
or *those that we sold*, if the noun is clear.

those kinds of ~s	CHANGE TO	that kind of ~, those kinds of ~

See the comments under *these kinds of ~s.*

those people who	CHANGE TO	those who, people who

As with *those* and *that*, to use both *those* and *who*
is to be doubly restrictive.
The solution is to cut *those* or to cut the noun
and have the adjective as a substantive pronoun:
those people who went should be *(the) people who went* or
those who went, if the noun is clear.

though	COMPARE	although
though	COMPARE	if

See the comments under *if.*

thus	COMPARE	therefore
thus	TRY	so

At the beginning of a sentence, *so* is less formal
than *thus* or *therefore*. Keep in mind, however, that
so is often overused as a conjunction.

thusly	CHANGE TO	thus
(at that point in) time	CHANGE TO	then, at that time, at that point
(at this point in) time	CHANGE TO	now, at this time, at this point
(changes over) time	CHANGE TO	changes
(period of) time	CHANGE TO	time, period
time period	CHANGE TO	time, period
(at the) time when	CHANGE TO	when
to + adverb + verb	TRY	to + verb, adverb + to + verb, to + verb + adverb

Seldom split an infinitive:
to needlessly split an infinitive should be
*to split an infinitive needlessly, needlessly to split
an infinitive*, or simply *to split an infinitive*.
Two uses of the split infinitive are unassailable:
if the adverb is more important than the infinitive, as
in *to blithely go*; if rejoining the infinitive makes
a sentence sound strange.

to a large extent	TRY	largely
to try and do	CHANGE TO	to try to do
to what extent	TRY	how much
..., to wit:	CHANGE TO	...:
together with	CHANGE TO	with
total ~	CHANGE TO	~
(a) total of	CUT	
totally	CUT	
toward	COMPARE	to
towards	CHANGE TO	toward

On the western side of the Atlantic,
the *s* has succumbed to the newspaper editor's pencil.

transmit	TRY	send
transpire [become known]	COMPARE	occur, happen

transportation	CHANGE TO	transport
trivial	TRY	small
try and, try to	TRY TO CUT	
try out	TRY	try
turbid [muddy]	COMPARE	turgid [swollen]
turgid [swollen]	COMPARE	turbid [muddy]
twice	COMPARE	double

See the comments under *double*.

type	TRY	kind
(oldest ~ of its) type	TRY	oldest ~ of its kind
(these or those) types of ~s	CHANGE TO	this type of ~, these types of ~, that type of ~, those types of ~

Note first that *type* should often be *kind*.
Note second that the plural is often unnecessary:
these types of ships should usually be *this type of ship* or
these types of ship. Some editors prefer to rescue the
noun from the prepositional phrase
by writing *ships of this type.*

typically	TRY	often, usually

U	**U**	**U**

ultimate	TRY	last, final
ultimately	TRY	finally, in the end
un~	COMPARE	in~, non~, not

See the comments under *in~*.

under consideration	TRY TO CUT	
underway	CHANGE TO	under way

The adjective *underway* is seldom used;
the adverb *under way*, as in *construction is under way*,
is almost always what is intended by *underway*.

undue (unduly)	CUT	

unfortunately	CUT OR CHANGE TO	but

The word should not be used more than once in a
manuscript, if that often, for it adds nothing.

unless and until	CHANGE TO	unless
(highly) unlikely	CHANGE TO	unlikely
unnecessarily	CHANGE TO	needlessly
until such time as	CHANGE TO	until
untimely	CUT	
(rely, depend, or insist) upon	CHANGE TO	rely, depend, or insist on
U.S.	COMPARE	United States

Spell it out, except as an adjective.
U.S. interests but *in the United States.*

usage	COMPARE	use

Usage refers to a manner of use—rough, for example
—or to a habitual practice that creates a standard, as in
language. *Use* should be used for all other uses.

useful	TRY TO CUT	
utilize (utilization)	TRY	use

The scholarly exception is to use *utilize*
for use against a standard, as in *capacity utilization.*
But *capacity use* conveys just as much.

V	V	V
(a) variety of	CHANGE TO	many, several, different
various	TRY TO CUT OR TRY	different
vast majority of	TRY	most
verbal [of words]	COMPARE	oral [of mouth]
versus [so as to face]	CHANGE TO	against, as against, relative to, compared with, in contrast to
very	CUT	
via	CHANGE TO	by, through, by way of
(the) viability of	TRY TO CUT	

viable [ability to live and grow]	TRY	lasting, practicable, workable
vice versa	TRY	the converse
(in the) vicinity of	CHANGE TO	near, about, close to
(in) view of	TRY	because
(in) view of the fact that	CHANGE TO	because
(with a) view to ~ing	CHANGE TO	to ~
viewpoint	TRY	view
virtually	CHANGE TO	nearly, almost
virtually all	CHANGE TO	most
(by) virtue of	CHANGE TO	by
vis-à-vis [face to face with]	TRY	compared with, relative to, in relation to
visualize	TRY	see, think of, imagine
volume [book]	CHANGE TO	book
(the) volume of demand for ~	CHANGE TO	the demand for ~

WXYZ   WXYZ   WXYZ

was	COMPARE	were

See the comments under *are*. For use with the
conditional, distinguish past impossibility (*if I was*)
and future possibility (*if I were to go*).

(in the) way of	TRY	in
(by) way of ~ing	CHANGE TO	to ~
we	COMPARE	I

Do not write *we* if you mean *I*.
In this book we will show should be
In this book I will show if there is one author.

(as) well as	TRY	and, also
were	COMPARE	was

See the comments under *are* and *was*.

whatever	CUT	
when	COMPARE	if, in which

when and if	CHANGE TO	if [possibility], when [temporality]
when the ~ was over	CHANGE TO	after the ~
where	COMPARE	if, when, in which
whereas	CHANGE TO	but, though
whereby	CUT OR CHANGE TO	so that
wherein	CHANGE TO	in which
wherewithal	CHANGE TO	means, money
whether	COMPARE	if

See the comments under *if*.

| whether or not | CHANGE TO | whether |

The *or not* often is not needed:
The managers are trying to decide whether
they should adopt the policy (or not).
In this and in many other constructions,
the *or not* can be dropped.

| which | COMPARE | that |

The important things are knowing why you use one or
the other and punctuating *which* clauses correctly.
See chapter 7.

| (of) which | TRY | whose |

Whose is a useful word that fills the gap
between *who* and *that*, a gap that too often is
infelicitously filled by *of which*.

| which is (are) | TRY TO CUT |

Try to delete *which is (are)* in a restrictive clause:
An item which is exported is the same as
but longer than *An item exported*. The same goes for
Factors which are deleterious to, which can be cut to
Factors deleterious to. Recall that the preference of this
book is to reserve *which* for nonrestrictive clauses.
Try, too, to delete *which is (are)* in a nonrestrictive
clause. Thus: *The plan, which is the first of many,...*
can be shortened to *The plan, the first of many,....*

whichever	TRY TO CUT	
while	TRY	when, although

Some writers follow the practice—and it is a good one
—of reserving *while* for clauses describing action
at the same time as the principal clause,
although for clauses describing opposing conditions.
If the subordinate clause follows the main clause,
while is not preceded by a comma. Thus:
He went to town, while she slept should be
He went to town while she slept if the meaning
of *while* is *during the time that.*
If the meaning is *and,* as in *He went to town, while she
slept,* change the comma to a semicolon and cut
while: He went to town; she slept.

(stay a) while	CHANGE TO	stay awhile

But stay *for a while.*

whilst	CHANGE TO	while
who	COMPARE	whom

It would be nice to settle the confusion in one sentence
but it is not that simple. The basic problem is that the
two words are so often confused in speech.
The most common errors are using *who* for *whom*
at the start of a question, as in *Who did they fire?*
and using *whom* for *who* in a nonrestrictive clause,
as in *The mayor, whom reporters said would be running for
reelection, was silent about his plans.*
Whom is correct in the first example, *who* in the second.

who is (are)   TRY TO CUT

Try to delete *who is (are)* in a restrictive clause:
A person who is going to France is the same as
but longer than *A person going to France.*
Try, too, to delete *who is (are)* in a nonrestrictive clause.
Thus: *New Yorkers, who are thought by many to be cold,...*
can be shortened to
New Yorkers, thought by many to be cold,....

whole [the adjective]   TRY TO CUT

Many writers unwittingly use *whole* to
modify something that is by definition whole:
throughout the whole country says no more than
throughout the country.

| (on the) whole | CUT | |
| whom | COMPARE | who |

See the comments under *who.*

(~ in) width	CHANGE TO	~ wide
will in the future	CHANGE TO	will
will take steps to	CHANGE TO	will
~wise	CHANGE TO	with ~, about ~

Especially in such atrocities as *electricitywise.*
There are some unexceptionable exceptions:
clockwise, likewise, lengthwise, and *otherwise.*

wish	TRY	want
With [in the sense of Given]	CHANGE TO	Because of
with a view to ~ing	CHANGE TO	to
with reference to	CHANGE TO	of, on, for, about
with regard to	CHANGE TO	of, on, for, about
with respect to	CHANGE TO	on, for, from, about
with the exception of	CHANGE TO	except
within	TRY	in, between

The change almost always improves a sentence.
Within should be used when the object
of the preposition is an area or space—
and as a synonym for *inside of,* as in limits.

| woman [as adjective] | CHANGE TO | female |

| Y | Y | Y |

(in the) year 2000	CHANGE TO	in 2000
(3) years of age	CHANGE TO	(3), (3) years
you	COMPARE	people

> The second person should be used only in giving
> advice or instructions or in writing a letter or
> memorandum to someone.

your(s) and   CHANGE TO   your, and yours

> See the comments under *her(s) and*.

Latin Words, Phrases, and Abbreviations

a fortiori [with even greater force]	CUT OR CHANGE TO	even more, more obviously
a posteriori [from the latter]	TRY	inductive(ly)
a priori [from the former]	COMPARE	prima facie [at first view]

> Some confusion arises because of the similarity
> of some meanings of the two phrases.
> *A priori* refers to deductive reasoning—
> from causes or self-evident propositions to effects;
> in this sense it is the opposite of *a posteriori*.
> *A priori* also means to be without examination or
> analysis. In this sense the phrase often is mistakenly
> used for *prima facie*, which means at first glance.
> The two phrases can act as adverbs or adjectives.

a priori	TRY	deductive(ly), presumptive(ly)
ceteris paribus [other things being equal]	CHANGE TO	other things being equal, all else remaining unchanged
cf. [*confer* = compare]	CHANGE TO	compare
circa [fr. *circum* = around]	CHANGE TO	at, in, about, around
cum [with]	CHANGE TO	and, with, combined with, along with being
e.g. [*exempli gratia* = by way of example]	CHANGE TO	say, for example
e.g. [for example]	COMPARE	i.e. [that is]
et al. [*et alia* = and others]	CHANGE TO	and others

etc. [*et cetera* = and the others]	CHANGE TO	and so on, and so forth
ex cathedra [from the chair]	CHANGE TO	by virtue of, by the authority of one's position
ibid. [*ibidem* = in the same place]	CHANGE TO	in the same work
i.e. [*id est* = that is]	CHANGE TO	that is
i.e. [that is]	COMPARE	e.g. [for example]
inter alia [among other things]	CHANGE TO	among others
ipso facto [by the fact itself]	CUT OR CHANGE TO	by that fact
mutatis mutandis [with the changes needed]	CHANGE TO	with the changes needed
n.b. [*nota bene* = note well]	CHANGE TO	note well
non sequitur [it does not follow]	CHANGE TO	does not follow
op. cit. [*opere citato* = in the work cited]	CHANGE TO	in the work cited
pari passu [with equal step]	CHANGE TO	at the same time, pace, or rate; hand in hand
passim [fr. *passus* = scattered]	CHANGE TO	here and there
prima facie [at first view]	COMPARE	a priori [from the former]

See the comments under *a priori.*

prima facie [at first view]	CHANGE TO	at first glance
q.v. [*quod vide* = which see]	CHANGE TO	for which, see...
sine qua non [without which not]	CHANGE TO	an essential thing
v. or vs. [*versus* = against]	CHANGE TO	against, compared with, in contrast to
viz. [*videlicet* = namely]	CUT OR CHANGE TO	:, that is

The best solution usually is to replace *viz.* by a colon.